Monologues from

The Last Frontier Theatre Conference

The Best of the 2009-2012 Monologue Workshop

Monologues from
The Last Frontier Theatre Conference

The Best of the 2009-2012 Monologue Workshop

By Laura Gardner
and Dawson Moore

Focus Publishing
Newburyport, Massachusetts

Monologues from the Last Frontier Theatre Conference: The Best of the 2009-2012 Monologue Workshop

© 2013, Laura Gardner and Dawson Moore
Focus Publishing/R. Pullins Company
PO Box 369
Newburyport, MA 01950
www.pullins.com

Text designed by Integrated Composition Systems, Spokane, Washington

Cover: Mark Robokoff performs Ron Pullins' The Dollartorium at the Last Frontier Monologue Workshop in 2012.

Cover photos by Ryan Adkins, courtesy of Prince William Sound Community College.

ISBN: 978-1-58510-630-1

To see available eBook versions, visit www.pullins.com

All rights are reserved. No part of this publication may be reproduced, stored in a retrieval system, or transmitted in any form or by any means, electronic, mechanical, by photocopying, recording, or by any other means, without the prior written permission of the publisher. If you have received this material as an examination copy free of charge, Focus Publishing/R. Pullins Company retains the title to the information and it may not be resold. Resale of any examination copies of Focus Publishing/R. Pullins Company materials is strictly prohibited.

Library of Congress Cataloging-in-Publication Data

Monologues from the Last Frontier Theatre Conference : the best of the 2009-2012 Monologue Workshop / by Laura Gardner and Dawson Moore.
   pages cm
 Includes index.
  ISBN 978-1-58510-630-1
  1. Acting--Congresses. 2. Monologue--Congresses. I. Gardner, Laura, 1951- II. Moore, Dawson. III. Last Frontier Theater Conference. IV. Title.
 PN2061.M66 2013
 792'.028--dc23
                            2013005462

Printed in the United States of America
10 9 8 7 6 5 4 3 2 1

0213W

The authors would like to thank the University of Alaska- Anchorage and Prince William Sound Community College for their continued belief in the importance of the Last Frontier Theatre Conference.

Table of Contents

Foreword   xi
by Marshall W. Mason

On This Book and the Last Frontier Theatre Conference   xiii
by Dawson Moore

Introduction   1
by Laura Gardner

Monologues for Women   5

Title	Age	
Daniel Guyton's *Where's Julie?*	15	7
Jonathan Minton's *The Monkey Virus of Mildred Valley*	15	8
Amy Tofte's *Roadmap of the Jilted Lover*	Late teens to early 20s	9
Judah Skoff's *Circus*	Teens to 20s	11
Cody Goulder's *The Halfway House*	Early 20s	12
Tom Moran's *Boundary*	Early 20s	13
Ryan Buen's *Now Boarding*	22	14
Kate Mulley's *The Tutor*	27	15
David Clark's *An Inexcusably Fantastic Theatrical Work . . .*	20s	16
Lillian DeRitter's *Discourse*	20s	17
Jerry D. McDonnell's *Back Home*	20s	18
Nicholas Walker Herbert's *Coming Clean*	20 to 30	19
Corey Ann Haydu's *Café Manhattan*	mid to late 20s	20
Rand Higbee's *The Interview*	20 to 30	21
Dennis Schebetta's *Green Eyed Monster*	20s to 30s	22
Daniel Damiano's *Maya*	20 to 40	23
Antoinette Winstead's *Refugee*	34	25

George Sapio's *Headstrong*	36	27
Schatzie Schaefer's *A Fabulous Coat*	30s	28
Scott Tobin's *Struck*	30s	29
Kavelina Torres' *Something In The Living Room*	30 to 40	30
Kenneth L. Stilson's *The Cow and the Milk*	30s to 40s	31
Ron Pullins' *The Boss is Dead*	35 to 55	32
Paul Brynner's *Pivot Point*	40s	34
E.J.C. Calvert's *The Bear (A Tragedy)*	40s	35
Judd Lear Silverman's *Faith*	40s	36
Jennifer Williams' *Sexual Fantasies*	40s	37
David Guaspari's *New and Selected*	40s to 50s	38
Linda Ayres-Frederick's *Years Later: I Smell the Rain*	Middle-aged or older	40
Rand Higbee's *Edith (that person in front of you at the coffee shop)*	50	41
Lois Simenson's *Glaciers and Demons*	Mid 50s	42
Karyn Traut's *Caffeine?*	50 to 65	43
Henry Murray's *Treefall*	60s	45
Jeanne Beckwith's *The Man in the Hat*	old	47
Kevin Six's *Integrity Problem*	Indeterminate age	48

Monologues for Men   **51**

Title	Age	
Ryan Buen's *Hey, Judae*	20	53
Tom Moran's *Boundary*	Early 20s	54
Dawson Moore's *Revenge Fantasy*	20s	55
David Clark's *An Inexcusably Fantastic Theatrical Work...*	20s	56
Cody Goulder's *The Halfway House*	20s	57
Nicholas Walker Herbert's *Teddy Berg's Story*	20s	58
Rand Higbee's *A Tribute to the Late, Great Bird*	25	59
Gail High's *Breathe In Breathe Out*	25	60
Laura Neubauer's *The Chasm*	mid 20s	61
Jonathan Minton's *Someone to Watch Over Me*	Late 20s/Early 30s	62

Eoin Carney's *'Course I Know Marcie*	30s	63
Melissa Gawlowski's *Spring Tides*	30s	64
Elena Hartwell's *The Last Train to Hicksville*	30s	65
Carolyn Kras' *The Virus*	30s	66
Michael Parsons' *Fire Dance*	30s	67
Henry Murray's *Treefall*	30s to 40s	68
Jeanne Beckwith's *Filmed in Bagdad*	At least 35	69
Ron Pullins' *The Dollartorium*	At least 35	70
Erica Silberman's *In the Night Everyone is Equal*	Late 30s	72
Arlitia Jones' *The Ugly Children of Eve*	Late 30s	73
Amy Tofte's *FleshEatingTiger*	Late 30s to 40s	74
Damon Chua's *Film Chinois*	30-50	75
Joe Barnes' *Father Francis Gives His Farewell Sermon*	Middle-aged or older	76
Al Frank's *Ain't No Place Like Home*	63	77
Jerry D. McDonnell's *Engines of Time*	Late 80s	78
Jaron Carlson's *Stalker*	Any age	79

Monologues for Men or Women — 81

Title	*Age*	
Allan Lefcowitz's *Colleagues*	40s or older	83
Barry Levine's *The Dreamer*	Ageless	85
Tom Moran's *Pac-Man*	Any age	86
Joe Barne's *October 18, 2009*	Any age	87

Index by playwright — 93

Foreword

The Last Frontier Theater Conference is one of the most dynamic opportunities for theater artists in the United States. Each summer for more than 20 years, playwrights, actors, and directors gather in Valdez, Alaska for a marathon of rich theater experiences. Fledgling playwrights have the chance to hear their work read by professionals, and evaluated with generosity and insight by distinguished playwrights, directors, and critics. Established with the guidance of playwrights like Edward Albee, August Wilson, Terrence McNally, and a host of other prominent writers, the conference focuses on the development of new work. It stimulates and inspires, and has become the event of the year for many theater artists.

As a director, I've not only been excited to encounter new scripts that deserve further production, it's also been my pleasure to work with two outstanding actors, Laura Gardner and Frank Collison, whose artistic excellence ranks them at the top of their profession. Their advice and supervision of actors at the conference are just as valuable and inspiring as the support and encouragement received by the playwrights.

The core of Laura and Frank's influence at the conference is contained in their Monologues Workshop, wherein they expand the skills that sharpen and deepen an actor's process. Both are not only talented performers, but also are consummate teachers of the actor's craft. The benefits of a week of concentration on perfecting the techniques of acting can hardly be overstated. The performance of the monologues on stage at the end of the conference is one of the highlights of each summer.

Marshall W. Mason
Founding Artistic Director of Circle Repertory Company
and author of *Creating Life on Stage*

On This Book and
The Last Frontier Theatre Conference

What you now hold in your hands, or are reading on the screen, is a collection of pieces that were a part of the Monologue Workshop from 2009 to 2012 at the Last Frontier Theatre Conference. I have had the privilege of coordinating the Conference since 2003, and in 2012 it had its 20-year anniversary.

This Conference is different from many other similar playwriting events across the country, primarily through the number of playwrights in attendance each year. 2012 was a small year at 48; we are usually around 60. Having so many authors presenting their work makes us less capable of developing everyone's individual play. Don't get me wrong: we work on the plays. But if we limited ourselves to 10 playwrights, we could spend all week focusing on their individual pieces.

Our authors receive one rehearsal with their cast before presenting the plays to an audience and panel of professional respondents. While I believe deeply in the value of the Play Lab experience, we are far more about developing the writers themselves. They share in each other's work in one of the more beautiful places on earth . . . they eat the same inadequate lunch, go to the same scary Alaskan bars, and journey to a glacier together on a late night cruise. They spend all week immersed in dramaturgical thought with other people who are willing to travel a long way to share in this conversation. In a week, they become a part of an artistic community that feels more like family.

There are few places where playwrights can come together and not be in competition with each other. The Last Frontier Theatre Conference is one of them.

To make a playwriting conference of our size happen, you need a lot of actors. The fewest we've had in a decade was 120. On our feedback forms, the overwhelming comment we kept hearing was that the actors wanted more to do. Reading in the Lab was great, but if someone only had 2 roles, that left them with a lot of free time.

The creation of the Monologue Workshop was an effort to address this.

Laura Gardner suggested that we get the authors presenting work in the Lab to create pieces for her to work on with actors. We decided to give it a whirl.

Playwrights whose work is accepted are solicited to send us monologues. We jury them, then post them on our website, and let actors choose from them, allowing up to two performers of each piece. They work with Laura and Frank Collison over two classes and a number of individual sessions by appointment. On the final day of the Conference, the actors present their work to the rest of the participants.

After doing this for a couple of years, and leaving the previous years' monologues available on our website, we began to build up a large collection of good material. Some of our past participants who teach acting began sending their students there to find material to work on.

On What Does (And Doesn't) Make A Good Monologue

During the Unknown Theatre Company's auditions for a series of one-acts they were doing in San Francisco, we saw about sixty people, and three of the men used the same piece, from Robert Anderson's 1968 gem *I Never Sang for My Father*. Three people, doing the same dated piece I'd seen many times before, trying to stand out as individuals.

Which leads me to the first aspect of a monologue I think is important: freshness. Not necessarily that it's a new piece, but if everyone's seen it before, there are negative consequences.

When you have multiple people performing the same piece at the same audition, only one of them is best, effectively eliminating everyone else who used that particular monologue. If you're doing a piece that's been out for years, you're competing with everyone else the casting powers have seen in the past ("I remember when I saw this done amazingly 15 years ago," is not something that should be thought by people paying attention to your audition!).

In college, I must've seen that piece from David Rabe's *In the Boom Boom Room* twenty different times. Years later in San Francisco, Naomi Iizuka's *Aloha, Say the Pretty Girls* seemed to be required at every audition. These are both GREAT monologues. They accomplish all the artistic things one is looking for:actors get to show range, and there are clear objectives, and the language is evocative . . . but every time an actress begins her piece with "All throughout my sophomore year in high school," I begin to think about how often I've heard the piece, how I'd find it more interesting if she was slathering herself with guacamole than butter, anything but "I wonder if I should cast this actress."

While I hope that this book becomes as ubiquitous as the volumes that popularized those two pieces, for the moment we're a more obscure source, and it's unlikely you'll find yourself up against multiple actors who've chosen the same monologue.

Assuming that you do find a piece that's not overdone, what else goes into making a monologue "good?" The same things that always make theatre good! One: Objectives. You don't want a passive story; you want a character who desperately needs something from another character, and will do anything to get it. Stories without strong objectives can provide actors with the opportunity to show their emotional honesty, but frankly, in a competitive auditioning environment, I think of that as kind of the minimum of the actor's craft . . . of course you can be emotionally honest and believable, or you wouldn't be in the room. If you can't, you won't be in it much longer.

Two: Range. A good piece will provide you with the opportunity to employ different tactics in pursuing your objectives. Sometimes pieces will sacrifice nuance for passion, and this can leave you giving a flat performance.

Three: Appropriateness to the audition. There's a reason they tell you to have multiple monologues in your bag of tricks. There is no "Best Monologue in the World," because there are plenty of auditions for which it won't help you get the role. We've got a wide variety of pieces in here, one for almost any contemporary audition you might be going out for. No point showing off your comedic chops if the play is a drama about rape in the military. No point in showing the depths of your soul to prove you can play the jester.

And the last thing: you should like it. And I mean really like it . . . if the phrase "good enough" enters your mind after reading it, you should probably keep reading. Find something about a monologue that you love, that moves you personally or makes you laugh aloud while reading it. Artists who settle for "good enough" rarely end up matching that description themselves.

The Obligatory Thanks

Very little happens in this world without the assistance of others, no matter what politicians may claim for temporary gain. Of course, this starts with the programs teachers, Laura Gardner with Frank Collison. They were the inspiration to start the program. They were my primary partners in refining the program over the years. They are both brilliant actors and acting teachers, and I love them.

Then there's the vague thanks to all the writers, actors, and technicians who've participated over the years. If you build something, but no one comes, well then, that thing doesn't last very long. I appreciate all their hard work.

Then there are my employers, Prince William Sound Community College, and my co-workers there. They make being the event's figurehead a pretty easy job.

Lastly, thanks to Ron Pullins for joining us as a playwright and being open to facilitating my proselytizing about the Theatre Conference, an amazing event in an amazing place.

I hope you enjoy work we've amassed here, and best of luck with your audition!

Dawson Moore
August 1, 2012

Introduction

I have been an actor for over 50 years and I have surely worked on that many monologues. The quest for the "perfect monologue" is the holy grail of any serious actor. It's also a prerequisite for anyone auditioning for an acting program not to mention something every professional actor should have in his hip pocket.

I am one of those people who love to perform and coach monologues because I think monologues are an opportunity for an actor to fully express her/himself . . . creating everything!!

I have been a featured artist at the Last Frontier Theatre Conference for the last six years. The first two years I focused on workshops that used Uta Hagen's teachings to prepare auditions for theatre, television, film, and commercials. I then started asking if anyone had monologues they would like to present. I also gave the students the option of writing a monologue. At this time I discovered that there were Alaskan theatre companies auditioning actors during the weeklong conference.

I had an idea: Let's pool our wonderfully talented resources.

Here we have at least 60 playwrights with new material over actors auditioning with material that has been heard before. Here was my idea: get the playwrights to contribute their material and the actors would have "world premiere" monologues with which to shine. That was the birth of the Monologue Workshop.

I believe this is the only place in the country that does this kind of workshop, one that focuses on original material, specifically matching the material to the actor. We discovered that there are added bonuses: the writers get the chance to work with us in the workshop and to see actors revealing the strengths and weaknesses of their writing. The playwrights will also have their work performed before other theatre professionals when the actors use their monologues in future auditions—a win/win situation.

Here is how the process works: a few weeks before the conference, the new monologues are posted on the Last Frontier Theatre Conference website. Actors choose a piece; no more than two can do the same monologue.

In preparation for our coaching, the actors are asked to memorize their pieces and do the preliminary work using the worksheet below.

THE PREPARATION

WHERE AM I?
   Time: year, hour, day, etc.
   Place: city, environment, room, outdoors

WHAT JUST HAPPENED?
   The given or imagined circumstances that happened just prior to the first beat.

WHAT DO I WANT?
   My overall objective in the scene

WHAT'S IN MY WAY?
   The obstacle

WHAT DO I DO TO GET WHAT I WANT?
   These are the actions of the scene (i.e. to fight for what I want, to plead, to demand)

Not only do the actors need to answer all these questions, they need to do a "Sherlock Holmes," mining who they might be talking to in their own life, using substitutions to strengthen their need. **Who you are talking to makes or breaks the work.** It must be someone that matters to you. Who you choose informs every choice you make.

These questions are based on the work I have done with Uta Hagen *(A Challenge to the Actor)* and Carol Rosenfeld of HB Studio in NYC; this is also what I teach at The Howard Fine Acting Studio in Los Angeles and Australia.

Although we call them monologues, they are in reality a scene in which only one of the characters (you) speaks. We explore with that idea in mind. What might the other person be trying to say or do? It is a fully alive scene that begins before the first line and will continue after the last line. If the actor can get the full script from the writer, many of the preparation questions will be answered. If the monologue is a standalone piece, the actor must create all the circumstances using their imagination. . You get to create whatever you need to be happening with your "partner" in order to stay in the room, to create the heat, to be present. **You can never be too specific!**

The workshop consists of two 90-minute segments where we guide the actors to make their most specific and personal choices, and where the playwrights can give insights and/or rewrites. Each actor then has at least one private session where we examine their unique connection to the material.

The work continues through the week in Valdez; sometimes I even coach actors on the boat trip which takes all our conference participants to Shoup Glacier the night before the presentation!

And then on Saturday morning the monologues are presented to a warm, enthusiastic audience which includes many of those Alaskan theatre directors and producers looking to cast their upcoming seasons. A joyful hour of new and exciting work, brought to life for the first time! Ah, the magic!

I am delighted to be a part of the Last Frontier Theatre Conference and to be the coach of the Monologue Workshop with the assistance of my husband, actor Frank Collison.

I hope you find something that works for you in this anthology! And join us at the conference!

Laura Gardner
www.lauragardner.org
www.theatreconference.org

Monologues for Women

From **Where's Julie?** By Daniel Guyton

JULIE: 15. Female. Rebellious teenager. Has just found out she's pregnant.

Dear Jesus, I'm sorry I called you a crock of shit. I just . . .
> *(She drops her hands onto the bed)*

I'm not very good at this. Praying. Talking to someone who isn't there. Or maybe you *are* there, Jesus. I don't know. But it sure doesn't seem like you care anymore. Is that what it is? You're there, but you just don't care anymore? Because that seems more likely if you ask me. Not that I blame you. I wouldn't care either if I was you. Here you are, dying for everybody's sins, and yet . . . here we all are—still sinning. People are terrible, aren't we Jesus? Allowing you to die like that? So . . . painfully . . .
> *(Pause)*

So here's the question of the hour, Mr. Jesus. Should I have this baby? Because wouldn't it be a *bigger* sin to bring him into a world like this? Full of . . . pain and agony? And what if he doesn't love me? What if I have this baby and he turns on me, the way we . . . most of us . . . have turned on you?
> *(Pause)*

I think I know how You felt now, Jesus. On the cross. Alone. Sacrificing *everything* for someone else. For everyone. Are you there? Jesus?

From **The Monkey Virus of Mildred Valley**
by Jonathan Minton

MARLENE: Teenage girl. Wide-eyed and optimistic, but a spitfire. Just recently ran her car into a Girl Scout stand to make national news

Okay, stop. Now look. I know what you're going to say, so you can just save it. What I did was wrong, I know that. But you know just as well as anybody, *better* even, that I've always wanted to be a star. And let's face it, Mama, Mildred Valley ain't exactly buzzin' with media attention, not like LA or New York or Minneapolis. We're a small town out in the middle of nowhere; people don't even know we exist. So when a whole buncha news crews show up because a rare strain of monkey virus breaks out at the hospital and the entire block has to be quarantined, well hell, I can't be the only one accused of getting all excitable. All those cameras, and the pretty women gettin' their hair done, *Matt Lauer*—oh, and Mama, you were right, he is a *lot* more handsome on TV—it was infectious. And I said to myself, "Marlene, now's your chance to be a star. Now's your chance to be a big name, like Sissy Spacek." Now, I know there are probably better ways to make the news than runnin' your neighbor's car through a police blockade and into a Girl Scout Troop's cookie stand. But I can hardly be blamed for not thinking straight, it's been a confusin' day. I mean, we have a monkey virus outbreak, when there ain't even any monkeys around? It just doesn't make sense! But at least no one was hurt, too much, and I'm sure that now them Girl Scout cookie sales are gonna skyrocket when people see how damaged their stand was—I mean, I know for a fact people buy junk food out of sympathy. And now everyone all over the country knows me as that Crazy Inbred Girl Who Ran Her Car Into a Quarantine Zone. No, it's not exactly the most flattering title, but it's a start. And mama, you have to understand, I was only doing what you've always told me to do—I was being true to myself. So, dammit, how can you ground me when I was only followin' your rules?!

From **Roadmap of the Jilted Lover** by Amy Tofte

GIRL: Late teens to early 20s. Young, innocent looking. Enters in a sweet school girl outfit . . .

Driving in the dark on slick wet streets:
Black, white and shiny—my heart pout, pounding.
Lights flash as onlooker hookers of the boulevard loiter
And stoop in my sideways vision.
My ears thump, thumping as I grip the wheel—
Change lanes, check the time, my phone, my face . . .
Should I call? Should I stop? I'm nearing his street.
Wait.
>   *(Beat)*

Was that him? So many cars,
I couldn't tell if it was blue or black.
I know his tail lights and glance back . . .
It wasn't him. My heart skipped ten raw beats.
It was my mistake . . . I know, I know. MY mistake.
I HAD to be honest.
I haven't actually shot anyone . . . no, that's not true.
I haven't KILLED anyone.
>   *(Beat)*

It's mostly for show . . . and good money. Better than babysitting.
They're just guns! And guns don't kill people! PEOPLE DO!
And when I get low on cash . . . I only hit 7-11's. They have INSURANCE!
It's like working free-lance selling . . . steak knives!
A steak knife could kill someone! I should have lied.
I HAD to tell him I was delivering semi-automatics the night we met.
>   *(Beat)*

Almost there. Almost to his street.
Turning left at the light . . . and my heart pout-pounding.
His street is narrow and lined with jumbled empty cars on both sides.
Someone already behind me with bright lights urging forward . . .
I want to drive slow. Real slow and see if his light is on.
I could drive slow, but they'll honk me up from behind and I don't want the attention. It was my mistake. My mistake. I HAD to be honest and up front.

But the headlights behind me. Keep moving, keep moving. No time to stop or slow or breathe . . . just slowly roll by the light in his window . . .
STOP PUSHING ME!
(Beat)
He drives a black Toyota Corolla. And I keep looking for him.
DO YOU KNOW HOW MANY BLACK TOYOTA COROLLAS ARE OUT THERE?!!
I only want a glimpse of him, see if he's home, if he's around, if he's still alive! See if he'll talk to me. I want to see . . . I want to see . . . I want to see . . .
(Beat)
Oh. He's not home.

From **Circus** by Judah Skoff

LAURA: Late teen to early 20s, ponderous and damaged.

My father found my mother in the back of a pickup truck with another man one hot night in early fall. Being of a forgiving nature, he took her back when she begged. Although reunion never guarantees reconciliation, and her fucking around continued. And it was with different men. And my father cared but couldn't find the strength to confront her.
(Beat)
He was a trucker and found no greater satisfaction than driving other peoples' goods across the plains. The kind of scenery that made his heart flutter was not a young blonde in a sundress, but rather an open field that never stopped.
(Beat)
My mother walked out on us both. I was ten. Maybe she felt guilty. Or maybe like some privileged teenage brat, she just felt tied down and had some inner need to break free. Then it was me and my father. Alone. He started taking me with him. I sat in the passenger seat of his truck and sometimes he let me pull at the horn or talk over the CB. He told me to watch out for the baser instincts of truckers. At the time I had no idea what he meant. Today I do. And that is how it was growing up. Some years later we learned that my mother ended up dead on the maroon carpet of a motel somewhere near the Texas-Mexico border. The police suspected that she was murdered. They even did some investigating. And I guess it was for show. Because no one cared. And they never found anyone. Nobody saw nothing. And besides they said, she was a boozer and a whore and a junkie. Why even bother with a prayer?
(Beat)
My father and I had long forgotten her. When we finally got the news we shrugged and maybe even felt sad for a moment. But then we looked out the window at the vast plains and prairies. We didn't know where we were, and we didn't care. We just liked the view. The great American heartland. We just liked the view. And we hoped that it would go on forever.

From **The Halfway House** by Cody Goulder

CASSIE: Early 20s actress; nostalgic.

My mother had been dead for almost three years and my dad was about it for me. For so long, I would see him sitting by the fireplace, his nose deep into some novel or newspaper and I'd always be wondering why he never went out. How he could just sit in the darkness and carry on. I remember getting so frustrated with him over it too. I missed my mother so much, and I couldn't understand how he could let the world pass by without so much as an afterthought. Then, he took me to see this play and, during the part where Romeo is forced into exile, I looked over at my dad and all I could see were the tears in his eyes. That's when I saw it, right then. All this time, he had wanted to break down. But, he couldn't because it's not how he wanted to remember her. Romeo vows to come back and he honestly believe he and Juliet will be together again. I started to forgive him that day and, from then on, my dad was always Romeo, waiting to be reunited with love. I know it may not make much sense, but R & J, to me, is my parent's story. And sure, they both die at the end, but through their love, they find a way to keep it eternal.
(Beat)
I've completely lost you, haven't I? Sorry.

From **Boundary** by Tom Moran

JESSIE: Female, early 20s.

You know why mom left, don't you?

She left because she ran this place by herself! Because you had all this big talk about living a self-sufficient lifestyle but you couldn't hack the self-sufficient part. And you wouldn't let her leave. And now you won't let me.

And no, you haven't held me here. You've just sabotaged every chance of me ever leaving. What was wrong with Travis?

The fact is, he was more of a man than anyone else who's ever come this way. And it scared you. So you found an excuse to run him off. And not just to run him off, but to kill him.

You sent him alone across twenty miles of godforsaken swamp and trackless forest on the verge of a snowstorm. It's ten below out there and it's getting dark. I bet he doesn't even have any food. And I bet the troopers aren't after him either.

Jesus.

You know what? I'm glad they're going to take this place away from us. Maybe someday they'll open it up as a little museum, and people will come here in tour boats and poke their heads inside this door and learn about you, and about what this life was like, and they'll get back on that boat and go back to their homes and hug their families and turn on their television sets and thank god for everything in their lives.

That'll be our legacy, daddy. What not to do.

From **Now Boarding** by Ryan Buen

RILEY: 22 year-old female. Effervescent and full of energy, if a little sad.

When I was a little girl, maybe seven, I asked my mother if I could have a pet. This is going somewhere I promise. She thought that a dog might be too much responsibility, so she decided to get me a fish. She took me to the pet store to pick one out . . . we spent hours there. I remember taking my time at each tank, watching the different fish, trying to make sure that I picked the right one, but I just couldn't make up my mind. I went from tank to tank to tank until finally . . . I found her. She was all kinds of beautiful colors. Red, blue, purple, gold. She swam around her tank like the queen of a castle, commanding respect from all of the other fish. I knew then, she was the one for me. We brought her home that day and put her in the tank all by herself. I told mom that I thought we should get some more fish to put in there with her, but she said that she didn't think I could handle that. "How can she be a queen when she has no one to rule over," I asked her. She just laughed. But the fish didn't, she just looked at me with those beautiful eyes of hers, defeated. Alone in that tank, all the life she had in her was gone. Then she got sick, she would just sit at the bottom of her tank all day staring out at nothing. Slowly it seemed as if her brilliant colors were beginning to fade away, every day she just seemed less and less the queen that she once was. I knew what I had to do. I ran to the kitchen, grabbed a cup, and scooped her up out of that tank. I saw my mother come running after me from the living room, but I managed to get outside before she could catch me. I took her to a lake nearby, and I let her go. Who knows how long she lived after that, but I swear, as that fish swam away it turned for a second, looked at me one last time, and said thank you. If I can't live how I want to, I'm at least going to die that way.

From **The Tutor** by Kate Mulley

MEREDITH: 27. Female. A tutor who leads a secret life online as "Cassandra," selling her used lingerie.

The last time I was home, I was put in charge of sorting through old boxes that had been labeled with my name. There may be nothing more damaging to the psyche than looking through papers of what used to be your life. Report cards, comments, programs from high school performances all in an unorganized pile or multiple unorganized piles spread around a room that has been transformed into a guest room/office. The seventh grade history teacher who broke my will at a critical point of my emotional development seemed just as frightening as he had been back in 1996. But what struck me the most were the notes that had been passed back and forth. The pieces of paper that had written conversations that couldn't be spoke aloud on during bus trips. The sweetly covert love letters from my first serious boyfriend. I sat on the floor laughing and crying at all of these documents from my past. It's harder to do that with an inbox of communication. You can't happen upon a hilarious text from your best friend in 9th grade ten years later. Or even one year later. You have to scroll through it. If it's even still there. I mean, I'm all for recycling and using less paper and saving trees, but it's weird to think that kids today won't have boxes of paper from their childhood to sort through just when they thought they had grown up.

From **An Inexcusably Fantastic Theatrical Work Featuring Everything There Is To Know About Love And Absolutely Nothing Less Than The Finest Use Of The English Language To Describe Events Most Romantical by Ethan Cross, title edited to Everything And Nothing by Constance Wright** by David Clark

JENNIFER: 20s. Female. Religious. Enjoys relationships with men who need to be "fixed."

But anyway, there I was watching and playing this video game with Eliot, I guess this was two nights ago, I mean, I've seen him every night this week... he's my best friend in the world after you. Hell, sometimes I think he might even be a better friend than you. But that's okay. Anyway, two night ago I just kind of leaned over as I was playing and realized suddenly how close I was to his face. And I thought, I could just kiss him. Just lean over and kiss him full on the lips. And it was so tempting, 'cause I was so alone, and he's just so nice. So nice to me. And always around. Not like you anymore. And then I realized the truth. I wasn't afraid of you leaving me. I was afraid of me leaving you. Afraid I wanted to end it. That I wanted someone else. So I sat awake all that night. I wanted so badly for him to ask me to stay the night. I just didn't want to be alone. And he didn't. He's such a nice guy that it probably didn't cross his mind. And then I realized that God was tempting me. I was being asked to make a choice between two men. And... well—I remembered what you told me once. We choose who we love. Love doesn't choose us. There is no perfect. No destined other. You were right. We must choose and I want to wake up every day, forcing myself if I have to, constantly choosing you. I mean, we've lasted for four years almost. It would be ludicrous to throw that all away on some sweet, innocent, good Christian boy who appreciates me, actually talks to me, cares about how my day went, and actually acknowledges I'm a living person when he's around me.

Discourse by Lillian DeRitter

WOMAN: 20s.

I know it feels good, and there's nothing wrong with it. And I'm not ashamed. I'm just feeling really used, you know?

A little bit of Voltaire here, a little bit of Kant there, a little Nietzsche in between.

I am sick of being your intellectual fuck buddy!

You ask, "What is your position on Libya" and all I hear is "position." When you say "body politic" all I'm contemplating is body. You don't even want to know what I'm thinking about when we discuss Foucault.

I want you to pay attention to something other than my excessively large . . . vocabulary. I mean look at these. Proust would stop talking for these and all you want to do is have discourse??

I love your shiny shiny mind. I love your back acne and your self-consciousness and the *terrible* jokes. I love all of you. So could you at least take a glance at all of me?

I want to talk to you in ways that get you excited as a body, not a brain. Let's be base and enact all of the sad, problematic clichés. And maybe, someday we'll be beyond the silly hegemonic markers manufactured by the romantic industrial complex and we won't have to hold hands waiting for the subway, or order for each other at restaurants. We won't have to stare into each other's eyes, hands clasped, blood diamond rings on our fingers. We won't have to devise elegant but dorky couples costumes for the yearly Halloween party or argue over when and how to buy a minivan. We'll always talk the way we do, because it's what makes me love you. But maybe we should experiment with other options, see how well we can argue when our tongues are otherwise occupied.

The discourse, baby, is great. God, you just blow my mind. So why don't we try blowing something else?

From **Back Home** by Jerry D. McDonnell

YOUNG WOMAN, late 20s. Wife of an Army veteran.

I can't take it anymore. Since he came home and took off that uniform he's . . . He doesn't talk for days and then he just stares at me. Or when he does talk he yells . . . or mumbles. Last night I reach for him. It's 3 A.M. He's not in bed. I find him in the kitchen. The frig door is open. He's sitting at the table drinking tomato juice. Cutting the arms off a Ken doll. He turned and looked at me. I ran. I ran clean out of the house. I swear I saw the fire of the devil in his eyes.

In high school he was the class clown, always laughing. Remember? I remember his smile. God, I miss that smile. I miss him. The only time he gets close to me is when he hugs me in bed after the lights go out. But then the sweats. The screams. I don't think he sleeps. Where did he go? What did they do to him? I'm afraid to go back home. I love him so much but he scares the hell out of me.

Coming Clean by Nicholas Walker Herbert

CHRISSIE: 20 to 30 years old.

(Chrissie sits next to Johnny, lying in a hospital bed.)
You awake? Good . . . Good to see you conscious.

You almost died last night.

You turned green, then blue, and then you stopped breathing.

I didn't know what to do, I thought you were gonna die. You still had the fucking needle in your arm when I found you. You had me so scared . . . hell, I'm still scared! I had to call them. So . . . here we are.

You can't keep this up anymore.

You need to stop what you're doing or next time, you'll die.

I know I said that we could drive up the coast, find a hotel, get some good stuff and cook it up, but we can't. I didn't want to face it, I thought I could work it out and make some kind of balancing act, but you can't manage anything when you're strung out on this shit.

I didn't want to admit anything, but know I have to now. You need to stop, so that *I* can stop. Please . . . I'm not as strong as you, Johnny . . .

But I don't want you to die, I don't wanna die either, and I feel like I'm dying right now, even though it's a gorgeous day out right now, I'm dying . . . And that's why . . . I can't take you home.

Your folks are gonna pick us up in a couple of hours, and they're going to take us to Sunset Clinic, and they'll help us get better . . . you can hate me for this, you can call me all the names in the book, and never see me or talk to me ever again, just so long as you come with me to Sunset. Otherwise . . .

We're not gonna make it. We're not gonna make it like this . . . we have to make a conscious effort to not let the monsters in our head take over . . .

All we have to do is . . . be brave . . .

Johnny? Please . . . I'm so scared . . . can you say anything?

Please . . . just . . . please . . . if you want to go . . . will you hold my hand?
(Johnny stares for a moment, then slowly takes her hand.)

From **Café Manhattan** by Corey Ann Haydu

ANNE: Mid to late 20s, quirky, smart and maybe a little drunk.

Is this what you want for me? Really? You want me to be with this guy here? Or do you just want me to be with someone? Do you just want me not to be single? Because it's starting to feel like it doesn't matter who it is, as long as I just find someone and settle down. Which is weird, right? Because you guys aren't settled down . . . not really. And maybe I'm just not ready to settle down. I'm still getting over Sam. And there's nothing wrong with that! Sam was great. I really loved Sam, so I don't have to be over him and date some weird guy you met once. Two years is not that long in the grand scheme of things. Two years is like two seconds. You know how many people I've slept with in a year and a half? Zero. And I can barely even tell! That's how short a year and a half is! That's right, NO SEX! You hear that Brett? You want to say something awkward and weird about that maybe? Want to suggest again that we have had sex? You know why I didn't mind you saying that to your date? Because for a minute I felt good. Like someone people would want to have sex with. I used to be someone people wanted to have sex with. Or, well I still am I guess, but it felt nice to pretend that I had actually had sex. It's like all the payoff without any of the stumbling around and putting on a condom and doing the walk of shame. Or . . . not all the payoff . . . whatever.

The Interview by Rand Higbee

RACHEL: 20 to 30 years old.

Experience in the fast food industry? Yes. A lot of experience. A great deal of experience. Lots of experience in fast food. Not actually working in fast food, but I've eaten a lot of fast food. I have certainly eaten a lot of burgers in my day.

And those uniforms your workers wear? I look very good in blue. Oh, yes. Blue is definitely my color. I should have worn blue to this interview. I kick myself that I didn't. If you saw me wearing blue? Interview over. I'm hired. Oh, and the hats! I've tried on your hats and trust me, I look cute. Really cute. It's like your hats were specifically designed to enhance my cuteness. If you want I could put one on and show you?
(She looks for a response.)
No? Well, I do look pretty cute. So. I eat burgers. I look good in blue. Cute in the hat. I'm guessing that's pretty much what you're looking for, right?

Oh, and I can count out change. I know a lot of people have trouble with that these days, but I am very good at counting out change. As long as the register is telling me how much to give back. It tells me to give back a dollar? I give back a dollar. It tells me to give back 25 cents? I give back a quarter. It tells me to give back 29 cents? I give back a quarter and . . .
(Counts on her fingers.)
And four pennies. Oh, and one more thing. If you have rules against dating a fellow employee? I'm your girl. I am your girl. Because trust me, I would never date a guy who works at a crappy little place like this. So! We good?

From **Green Eyed Monster** by Dennis Schebetta

SUZY: 20s-30s. Female. A housewife.

(Suzy and her husband, Frank, have just made love and are sharing intimate fantasies about who they sometimes think of when they make love to each other. Suzy has told him Paul Newman, and Frank reluctantly tells her but only if she promises not to get jealous.)

I'm sorry, what? Miss Piggy?! That's who you think about when we make love? That's so . . . so . . . bizarre! While the two of us are locked in a passionate embrace I'm imagining Paul Newman's gorgeous blue eyes and you're fucking a puppet? And are you Kermit the Frog in this fantasy? No, I said I wouldn't get jealous! Of course, I'm upset! Do you have a fondness for Porky Pig, too? So, what is this, a pig fetish or a puppet thing? Or is it the oddity of the idea that gets you off? Am I not kinky enough for you, Frank? If there's something you want me to do in bed, you just have to tell me. We never do anything exciting. Day after day it's the same old thing. So, maybe this is a message to do something crazy. Let's work this kinkyness out of your system. You and me. Right now. Let's go in the kitchen and get wild. We'll use an egg beater in indescribable ways. Let's have sex on the kitchen floor smothered in strawberry jam! No, we'll get too sticky. Butter! Smothered in butter! Let's make love in a way no one has ever imagined before. You want dirty? I'll do it. You want bizarre? I can do bizarre. Please, Frank. I want to be your Miss Piggy. C'mon, I'll grab the butter.

From **Maya** by Daniel Damiano

MAYA: Woman, 20s to 40s.

(Maya sitting at a table in a Friday's Restaurant. She is smiling. A moment.)

I do. Really. I'm looking at you and all I can think of is how lucky I am. Really. I'm being totally honest, so don't feel that I'm . . . you know, that I'm just telling you what you want to hear. I'm not. I mean, you know me enough to know that, right? So . . . yes, honestly . . . I really do.
(Slight pause)
I mean . . . of course, there are things that you . . . sometimes do. Little tendencies. I mean, they're so minor, that it's really trivial to address it in the larger scheme of. . . . But . . . there are . . . little things that . . . you do . . . that, you know, I'd like for you to work on. Again, minor, but . . . they're there so. . . . Well, just for example, you have a tendency to let your nose hairs grow a bit too long. I mean, again, it's nothing severe, but just something that I have addressed with you before which . . . you've chosen to ignore, and now I'm looking at you and revealing my love for you while you have the equivalent of wheatgrass emanating from your nostrils. It's just . . . a little distracting. But, again . . . minor.
(Slight pause, a strained smile.)
And just sort of . . . dovetailing on that, I wish you didn't act like you didn't hear me when I've made suggestions to you, like the nose hairs. Or, for that matter, you talking on top of me when we're with friends, which I've also . . . mentioned to you on several occasions. You know, how it always seems that I'm five words into a sentence before you jump on top of me, and end up speaking so loud that you completely drown me out, which really drives me . . . But, again . . . And, my God, you don't understand poetry that doesn't rhyme, and you fart in bed, and you have no sense of culture or taste or decorum. . . . and those fucking nose hairs!!! **My God, I can't even look at you. How can you not notice that?!!! They're like branches, for Godsakes! I mean, I almost want to climb up them and into your skull and punch your brain and scream; "TRIM THESE GODDAMN NOSEHAIRS, YOU FATUOUS, RIGHT-WING, FARTING PIG!!!!"**
(Slight pause, emotional but somewhat calm.)

Yet you still wouldn't hear me. But . . . you'd still ask me to love you . . . like you are now.

    (Slight pause, a sincere smile.)

And I do.

From **Refugee** by Antoinette F. Winstead

NADIRA MARIAL: 34 years-old. Black, Christian Sudanese ex-patriot. Refugee camp nurse.

(Setting: Present day. African refugee camp. She is speaking the chief physician of the refugee camp, a man who cannot understand why someone who loves children as much as she does, has not remarried and had children of her own.)

Do not lecture me on something you have no way comprehending. You are like the rest, sadistically probing old wounds until they bleed again. You want to understand, so you can help, change the way people think in this society? You're purposing a revolution in thought for an entire culture. In this part of the world, where machetes are still the weapon of choice? I am a realist, Doctor. Those eleven girls who came to camp today, it will take years of therapy to heal them, therapy they will probably never receive and even if they do receive it, there is no guarantee they will ever be at peace. Regardless, they have been tainted and will never ever be able to marry. Those are the facts, and that is the reality for thousands of girls and women just like them. It is my reality too. But you, you say I'm too remarkable a woman to be held captive by my past. What you consider my past is my present and my future. It is all I am and all I will ever be. . . . Yes, I have achieved much in my life despite what was done to me, but that does not mean that I am not reminded daily of my loss by this!
 (Nadira lifts her blouse revealing a hideous scar across her lower abdomen.)
This is my daily reminder, what holds me *captive* to my past.
 (pause)
They held me for days—I don't know how many. They beat me. They raped me. And when I became too disgusting for their use, they cut my baby from my belly and left me for dead. Does that educate you, help you to understand why a *remarkable* woman like me stays here, does what I do, is not remarried? Where would I go? What would I do? Who would marry this? Who could bear it, knowing what it means? *I cannot.* Sometimes, I bathe in the dark so I do not have to see it, but still I can feel the scar beneath my fingers. It is inescapable. But people like you would have me be-

lieve it is possible to heal, forget, and move forward. My body has healed, and I have moved on with my life. But this, this scar does not allow me for one moment to forget.

(Silence. Nadira lowers her blouse and starts to tuck it in.)

I am here because I have to be, because there is no other place for me.

From **Headstrong** by George Sapio

MIXIE: Female, 36-ish, desperate.

Let me explain a few things here. I'm not in love with you. I love Norman. With all my heart. I wasn't planning to fall in love with him. Handsome, charming, witty, clever. He was the worst thing that ever happened to me. Norman Miller barged into my life without even asking and my life walked away because I let it. He recited hours and hours of poetry to me, sent me flowers, wrote me letters every day. It was a blitzkrieg of romance. I was completely overwhelmed. I started to let the important things in my life slip away. After a year with Norman even the science lab microscopes couldn't find my grade point average. But Norman became everything. I hate myself for it. Today was his first day at a new job and I left work early, went shopping for things for his favorite meal because I wanted to congratulate him . . . and he came home at lunch to write another of his lousy goddamn stories and never went back. And he believes he did the right thing, that his fucking story was worth more than his new job. Ted, we are broke. I can't support us . . . and he doesn't care. And I can't leave. I can't leave because he'll always be there. I know he'll always be somewhere, Ted. He'll be breathing, cursing, quoting, getting the last word in every single time, making everyone around hate him, despise his arrogant, superior attitude. Every day I'll know exactly what he's doing. Every second. He'll either be brushing his teeth or typing or sitting in his goddamn chair reading who knows what. And I'll know it, Ted. Every second of every day. And he'll be easy to come back to. All I'd have to do is walk right through the door. He'll be haunting me by being alive, so he has to be dead. Then he'll be gone. Then I can't ever come back and I'll have to move on. Then I'll be alive. I won't be able to live until he dies, Ted. He has to die. He must die.

From **A Fabulous Coat** by Schatzie Schaefers

KATIE: A woman in her 30s, attractively dressed.

I have a curse. I'm not kidding. I don't know where it started but with this curse I get ignored in public. One time I went into this little jewelry store to have my watch battery replaced. I went in, there was this blonde lady working in the store. She was the only one there. I gave her my watch, she wrote up the order, I complimented her on what were actually some ugly earrings . . . giant, wooden things, just hideous . . . she mentioned that she picked them up in Uruguay . . . and she told me to come back in an hour and a half and my watch would be ready. So I went to lunch, did a little shopping, and came back. I walked in, there she was, same lady. Still the only person in the store. And I asked her about my watch. "I'm sorry," she said. "Someone else must have taken your order. What day did you come in?" I told her I was just there ninety minutes ago. She said that's not possible, since she's the only one working today besides the jeweler, who is in the back. I mention the earring conversation. I tell her she got them in Uruguay, and she looks at me like I'm some crazy person who's been spying on her. Perhaps I even followed her to Uruguay because that scenario is more believable to her than the possibility that we really did meet only an hour and a half ago. And that I really did give her my watch. Finally, I'm saved by a deus ex machina in the form of the jeweler, who comes out from the back and hands to me my watch. "Is this yours, Ma'am?" The blonde lady is completely befuddled.

(Katie walks, runway style, modeling her fabulous faux fur coat.)
But everything's changed since I got the coat. "Can I get you anything else?" "Would you like help out with those?" "Would you prefer a booth or a table?" People treat me differently in this coat. Even when I wear it over jeans. More attentively. With respect.

(Pause)
I just wish I could do it without the coat.

From **Struck** by Scott Tobin

SYLVIA: 30s.

I wonder what Mike would think. Mike, that's my husband. He'd find it devastating, of course. Let's face it. I'd be shunned. Banished from suburbia. Tossed out of the lawn-kingdom for my wanton desires. And what about Bradford? He'd wonder what happened to his mother. I mean, of course I'd still be his mother. He accept it after a while. Isn't that what kids do? Learn to accept things? We all learn to accept changes after a while. You and I could find a little place. A cozy studio in the village. Throw rugs and tiny lamps. A mattress on the hardwood floor. Ecru walls and African figurines on the shelves. Cooking fresh pasta with Sauce crème. Glasses of Zin while we languish on the fire escape. Fall nights and the makeshift gardens below us, with Christmas lights hung way too early. Wait. What the hell am I talking about? You haven't even opened your eyes and I'm setting our wedding date. I can't do this alone. I need you to tell me. Give me something. Anything. I need you.

From **Something in the Living Room** by Kavelina Torres

CORA ALICE: 30-40. Female. Gun for hire. Wears yellow opera gloves.

I was brought up as a proper young lady. But you know there is boredom in sameness. I spent some time in a slaughterhouse. A small one. Disguised as . . . as a man. I learned so much. I have seen what a body can do and what a body can take. Learned new ways to prolong a kill.
(Beat)
I wanted so much for my life. I was so practical . . . I had a microscope by the time I was seven. Well I stole it, but it was still mine. My sperm donor dragged me out from under my bed one night. I was studying parasite reaction to . . . doesn't matter. He clutched my legs, I clutched my microscope and then he threw it out the window. I fixed him, though. It took more than a few times but he received his just due. Maybe next time he won't touch my things. Well there won't be a next time.
(Beat)
My egg donor moped and moaned after him for months. It gave me time to brush up on my learning. By the time I was 14, I had set my heart on being a biologist. Until Ms. Stokes and Mr. Pander. Did they think I didn't hear? That I was deaf? They feared me. Perhaps I was a little cold but distance is a scientist's tool. How was I to know that Jimmy would scream so much? And it was his fault. You can't stamp out napalm.
(Beat)
Idiot . . . The talk is that Mr. Pander married Ms. Stokes and they ran off to Mexico. That's the talk.
(She gives a secret smile)
I changed towns. Changed family. Changed schools. Now as I sit here with my cucumber sandwiches and sweet tea, I want my fee without any hiccups or excuses. I just cleaned my guns and my knives are sharp. Sure hate to waste all that work on you. Am I as clear as the morning fog?

From **The Cow and the Milk** by Kenneth L. Stilson

BONNIE: 30s to 40s.

(Working on her daughter's prom dress)

Oh Boone, I want this to be the perfect night for our little girl. She has certainly gone through a rough patch after bein' fired from the Walgreen. I still cannot imagine why anybody would falsely accuse that child of stealin' all that stuff.
(Sighs)
Oh well, I feel like that's all behind her now. Tonight, she's gonna be like Cinderella just after the prince waltzed into her house and put that glass slipper on her foot.
(Holding the dress in front of her)
She is gonna look so beautiful tonight.
(Dancing in front of Boone)
Can you believe this used to fit me? Cain't ya see me dancin' at the ball? You remember our prom night? I had on this very dress. You had that hair. I swear ya looked just like Jon Bon Jovi. That bullhorn in the backseat of yer car pokin' me in the back. That was the night our little Marybeth was conceived. Of course, that was before my Prince Charmin' turned into a great big toad. Now look at me, Boone. I wan'cha to git yerself together. This is Marybeth's big night, and I wan'cha to make a good impression with her little friend. Don't say nothin' that's gonna embarrass her. Don't go talkin' politics. You always git into it with every person that walks in that door. Glenn Beck this and Rush Limbaugh that. Ya just never shut up about it. Nobody else can have an opinion around you. And I don't wan'cha talkin' about religion neither. Not everybody in this world is good Christians like we are. Just talk about cars. All boys like cars. Or sports. Talk to him about Dale, Jr. Everybody sure loved his daddy.
(Calling offstage)
Marybeth! Marybeth, ya better hurry up in there. Yer gonna be late for the ball!

From **The Boss Is Dead** by Ron Pullins

WACKOFF: 35-55. Female. She is in control. The corporate cookbook is the most sacred writing.

(The night manager is being chewed out by the supervisor who has visited the Interburger hamburger stand and found the situation not up to par. She chastises him by giving him a brief lesson on the perfect fry.)

These are not my French fries. These are not even French fries. And this stuff, Mr. Mann, running from these cold soggy "things" down my hand. What is this?

(Beat)

This is no longer shortening, Mr. Mann. This is grease.

(WACKOFF shakes her head)

The perfect fry, an Interburger fry, is perfectly frozen, then dropped immediately—full frozen—into shortening of the exact temperature to sear the outer layer of the potato, Mr. Mann, to scald it, seal it shut. Nothing escapes, nothing in, nothing out, and inside this fry the moisture is trapped—moisture that cannot escape, cannot leave, finds the front sealed, the back sealed, both sides closed in, trapped in this oppressive heat, Mr. Mann, and the heat rises, rises, turns suddenly to steam—purifying, scalding steam that races the length of the vegetable, and back again, but there is no escape. We are precise about what we want, Mr. Mann, so there is no error possible, no error at all, and only one outcome—the perfect fry. Foolproof.

(Beat)

Mostly foolproof.

(Pause. Her tone drops)

Unless, and only unless, we have a manager who fails to change the . . . grease. We have precise instructions, Mr. Mann, in the manual, do we not, about our shortening, and we explain, is it not true, that shortening, over time, after frequent cooking, after so many fries and frost and water and time, even the best shortening no longer seals the fry instantly, traps the moisture, keeps the shortening out. Instead, fries in old shortening, worn out shortening, are boiled until they are like so much spaghetti.

(Pause)

Boiled fries, Mr. Mann. Soggy, greasy, limp fries. Grease-that-runs-out-when-you-squeeze-them fries. Grease that runs down my hand, Mr. Mann. Greasy limp-dick fries, Mr. Mann, like these. Like yours.

From **The Pivot Point** by Paul Brynner

CAMI: A woman in her 40s, upper middle class, wife of an astronaut, talking to her best friend Nicole.

Let's get one thing straight. Your husband is a prick. Leaving him is the right choice. I don't care how sick he is. Phillip has become an utter prick. I feel liberated to say that now. He came onto me once, you know. Stuck his hand right up my skirt. There are lots of men who think that just because my husband is an astronaut I must be . . . what's the word? Lonely. Desperate. It's not true. I'm never lonely. I see my husband in every starry sky.
(pause)
He stuck his hand right up my skirt.
(pause)
And he set it right there. Right on my thigh.
(pause)
You were right there with us at the table when it happened. They'd seated you across from us. At the Andersons' Fourth of July picnic.
(pause)
I would have hit him right in the kisser if you hadn't been there. But you were. So I didn't react.

From **The Bear (A Tragedy)**[1] by E. J. C. Calvert

DIANE: 40s.

You went hunting this morning, didn't you. Early. I know, so don't you lie. Hunting for deer? Rabbits? No. No, you weren't. I saw your clothes when you got back—soaked! You'd jumped in that river again, I could tell. You'd been after those salmon. You can't catch salmon, Everett, you're a person! You're a human being! You haven't got any claws, you've got—you've got other things instead, fishing poles.

Do you want a divorce, Everett?

I'm trying to be serious. I loved you as a person. I don't need you to be all like that, all a bear and all. You were better before. Back then, you'd've never thrown the trash everywhere, or slept outside. You'd've never killed Mrs. Henn's golden. Then you lied to me and said it was your testes! I am not doing dishes anymore. I can't believe you, Everett, I thought you knew better than to run around killing innocents, I thought you'd changed since we moved out here! But now you're just a stupid hunter who I'm stupid married to. Jesus! I just wanted a nice quiet life in the Adirondacks. Is that too much to ask you? Stupid! And you have to go hunting! Stupid! You know how I feel about hunting.

---

1 By special arrangement with Samuel French, Inc. For performance rights please contact Samuel French Inc./Baker's Plays, www.samuelfrench.com.

From **Faith** by Judd Lear Silverman

GRACE: A middle-aged woman on a spiritual quest

Sister Ruth used to tell us it was a sin to question God. That God just is, you accept that on faith, you don't question it, and that that was true belief. I didn't understand. Granted, I was eleven years old at the time, but still, he wouldn't make his own existence such a mystery if he didn't want us to question it! I mean, everyone likes a good mystery, don't they?! Sister Ruth said "It's hardly up to an evil-minded little brat such as yourself to search out God's existence. He's there and you just have to open your heart and soul to him." "But not my mind, Sister?" "God's not interested in your mind, child." If God loves me, how could He not be interested in my mind? "Until you learn the true meaning of faith, child, you're going to the Devil." And so I've spent many years looking—since the day Sister Ruth told me I'd go to the Devil. Oh, yes, I believe there is good in the world. And there most certainly is evil. It encourages apathy, to look the other way, not to question. Kind of like Sister Ruth's faith, come to think of it. And I do believe there is a supreme being of some sort out there: anarchic but wonderful. But I don't believe I can't question it. If I were God, I wouldn't want the questions to stop. Faith is the belief that there are answers out there, even when we no longer can put words to the questions. I hope cranky old Sister Ruth's faith served her well, but frankly, I want to be more involved in my own salvation.

Sexual Fantasies by Jennifer Williams

MADGE: Female. A 40-something housewife. She may have a few extra pounds on her.

Well, I have one . . . where I'm in a bar . . . and I'm dancing . . . and this man sort of comes up to me, well, sidles up to me . . . no, no, that sounds seedy . . . he sort of swaggers up and moves in close and . . . holds me—he doesn't say anything—just holds me. And he's this sweet mix of beer and smoke and sweat. . . . And, well, anyway, somehow we get outside and my undies and stockings are around my ankles and he's pushing me against the wall . . .

Or, there's the one where I'm sort of lost in the woods, and it's raining? So, my dress has gone . . . see-through and sort of clingy, and this rugged, muscular man rides up on a horse . . . cliché, right? Is that bad?—he jumps off, and kind of . . . pushes me into the mud. He doesn't say anything . . . there's not much talking in these, is that normal?

They aren't particularly . . . feminist. I mean, I was all for the sexual revolution . . . I still am all for the . . . But, it's like my . . . libido is stuck somewhere in Mills and Boon.

And I don't read those books.

There's also the one . . . outside a church . . .

I'm not really sure I want to go into that one, actually.
Having fantasies isn't the problem.
(beat)
I think, really, the problem from my point of view, or, the . . . the . . . issue . . . or, I don't know, the "talking point" . . . is that none of them seem to involve . . . my husband.

From **New and Selected** by David Guaspari

MELANIE: 40s to 50s

(Melanie, at the lectern, beams at her audience.)
Thank you, Morris, for that introduction, which was so generous and so kind and—wow, "consciousness of a generation," that was heavy, that's a row to hoe, but thank you very much indeed.

And thank you all for coming tonight, when you might have stayed home to compost, or recycle tires into sustainable footwear, or find some other way to help heal Mother Earth. Which is not to lay a guilt trip on you. Just the opposite, because we are on a mission: To keep poetry alive. A mission urgent to all of us—except, possibly, the heterosexual males. But even if you're just tagging along with some chick you're trying to nail, I say, Welcome. If you're not part of the problem you're part of the solution.

Thanks also to the Macbeth Foundation for awarding me that Near Genius Grant. The $250 has purchased tonight's lovely light refreshments and made it possible for Morris to publish this limited edition of *New and Selected Poems of Melanie Palomar*—
(She displays a slender paperback.)
—though, as you can see, the selecting had to be pretty severe. A couple of C-notes stretches only so far.

And how nice to see familiar faces, including—Hi, Rainbow!—some of my students from the Melanie Palomar Academy of Verse and Martial Arts. Yo, Mongolia! And my man, D'Artagnan!

Those who don't know me may be wondering: Who is this person? This strange being? This poet? Excellent questions, addressed on every one of my Macbeth applications. And the answer to all of them is the same: *New and Selected Poems of Melanie Palomar*. Because, like all poets, I am my words—ever since I was a little girl filling notebooks with stories about the island kingdom of Melania and its magical princess Melona, who was stolen from the royal nursery by a family that made me grow up in a suburban development. Hang onto your misery, I tell my students—it's what makes you *you*.

New and Selected begins with my first mature achieved poem, which has a dreamy idealism I've never outgrown—and I couldn't be more glad about that. It's called "Fuck you, Pigs of the Power Structure."

(She reads)

    Fuck you, pigs of the power structure!
    See how you like the worm's course-correction,
    The other-shod foot,
    The day-having dog.
    Fuck *you* Fuck *you*!
    Pigs
    Of the Power Structure!

Can you say, lightning in a bottle?

From **Years Later: I Smell the Rain**
by Linda Ayres-Frederick

WOMAN: Middle age or older.

What if we had kept the boy—if it were a boy—that we got rid of so succinctly in Paris? . . . My choice . . . He left it up to me . . . lapsed Catholic that he was . . . but knowing what lay ahead . . . knowing deep in my bones that he would not last . . . that I could not . . . cannot . . . see him fathering a child of mine when he could barely step-father those I have . . . that there was . . . is. . . . no way in hell that I'm going to give birth to another one. I had . . . have no choice.

So, I go through with the procedure . . . that grey December day . . . without anesthesia . . . terrified to go under in a foreign country or any country but certainly not a foreign country . . . and I felt . . . feel . . . my insides being burned . . . cauterized . . . sucked out of me. I'm on fire, burned alive from the inside out digging my finger nails into the palm of the attending nurse who whispers to me as the valium wears off before the *medicin* arrives, that older nurse of experience . . .

(whispering in a French accent)
"Next time". . . . What next time? There isn't going to be a next time. . . . "Next time, ask for a different physician . . . Ask for one who knows how to use the local anesthesia . . . Ask." . . . But I don't know how to ask . . . My legs are already spread open in the stirrups . . . I don't know how!

Later that evening after the removal of the fetus, we walk . . . artist and his adoring model . . . up from the Metro . . . into a confusion of umbrellas amid a mob of women with placards protesting against the anti-abortionists . . . fighting for the right to determine what is done to their own bodies . . . fighting for the right of choice which I had just exercised . . . and I kept . . . keep wondering . . . Did I make the right choice?

From **Edith (that person in front of you at the coffee shop)** by Rand Higbee

EDITH: A woman of 50, studying the options at Caribou Coffee.

Is it me? Oh, my. I don't know what I want. So many choices. Caribou Coffee. Caribou Coffee. Why do they call it Caribou Coffee? Moose Coffee doesn't sound so good, does it? I don't believe I would want a Moose Coffee.

Oh, look. Caribou Coffee has tea. Many kinds of tea. Earl Grey tea. English breakfast tea. Cinnamon spice tea. However, I do not like tea. So I will not be having tea.

Trivia. "Answer the question; save ten cents." That sounds fun. "What was Mount McKinley before it was Mount McKinley." I assume it was still a mountain, wasn't it? I do not know the answer to that question. I guess I will not be saving ten cents.

Let's see. A mocka. I believe I will have a mocka. But look at all the many kinds of mockas. Turtle mocka. Campfire mocka. White chocolate mocka. Is there such a thing as just a plain old regular mocka? I believe that's what I'll have. A plain old regular mocka. So many choices. I will have that hot. And large. That is how I would like my mocka.

Wait a second. I didn't know you had cocoa. I like cocoa.

From **Glaciers and Demons** by Lois Simenson

ROSIE: Mid 50s. Overachiever, but still fell short of goals. Undergoing mid-life crisis.

I've dreamed of being in movies ever since I can remember . . . but life always got in the way. I didn't do drama in high school, I thought the drama kids were geeks . . . instead, I partied. Wished I would have now . . . it might have led to a movie career *and* saved my brain cells. Even if I failed, at least I could say I tried. Don't you hate regrets? Failure isn't as frightening as regrets. Life isn't fair . . . we get our big chance . . . then whack . . . we wind up on the cutting room floor, and tossed in the dumpster like we never mattered. I made other choices . . . cashed in dreams for reality. Why do we do that? I'm just another humiliating statistic . . . one of millions, walking around the planet . . . shoulda, woulda, coulda . . . I wish I had a do-over. I always wonder if I would have made the big time. At least I could have been an extra. Now I'm just a hot-flashing, mood-swinging, forgetful, never-was. So, *this* is what a mid-life crisis is like . . . It's bad enough not being young anymore.

(Looks down, lifts both breasts, they fall back into place)
My biological clock not only ticked, it spit out its batteries. My only hope is to do little old lady roles, like Ruth Gordon . . . I could do a remake of *Harold and Maude*.

Caffeine? by Karyn Traut

WOMAN: 50-65. Female. Confident, strong, able to stand up for herself. Monologue has left her humbled.

So, people wonder about this aging thing. Well—it's really affecting my husband. He needs hearing aids now but he won't wear them because he feels he's too young. He only wears them when he's teaching so he can hear his students. He won't wear them when we're alone together because it's his idea that I always talk too softly so if he can't hear me, it's my fault and not his lack of hearing.

He misses consonants—he's been tested and shown that consonants are in the high and low registers and he can only hear in the middle. So he can't distinguish "hat" from "bat." You can imagine the amusing exchanges we've had.

My hearing has been tested to be perfect.

The other day I had breakfast with one friend, then later that afternoon, because my husband and I were going to be gone for a month, I planned a coffee after yoga class with another friend. Before we went in I said: "Let me call my husband to tell him I'll be later than usual."

His response caught me off guard: "Isn't that a lot of conversation for one day?"

"What? I haven't seen Melody in three years and this is the last chance I can see Sandy before we leave."

"Okay," he seemed to shrug, "if that's your choice."

I thought: "What is going on with him? Conversation is good for my morale. When has he ever before tried to confine my friendship hours?" Aging had to be the answer.

I was tired after the full day so went to bed early. At 1:00 a.m. I awoke. By 2:00 I was still awake so rose, did some work, then tried unsuccessfully to go back to sleep.

At breakfast I was groggy. I explained that I'd been awake for some reason from 1:00 until 4:00, so I was going to have a rough day while we were packing.

He offered: "I tried to warn you but you wouldn't listen."

"You told me I was having too much conversation. Conversation is stimulating but it's never kept me awake at night before."

He looked at me very calmly: "I said: 'Isn't that a lot of caffeine for one day?'"

"Caffeine?! You said 'caffeine'?!"

"Yes."

"You said 'conversation.' I heard you say I was having too much conversation for one day. If I'd heard caffeine I would have remembered to order decaf!"

He: "It's not my fault if you're hard of hearing."

I don't complain about his hearing anymore.

From **Treefall** by Henry Murray

MAE: A retired school teacher who has become a treesitter.

> *(After her husband's death, Mae was obliged to sell their house. She took a road trip to Northern California and through a complicated series of events ended up joining a group of tree-sitters doing battle with a logging company. This speech is delivered to the audience from her perch in a Redwood.)*

George was a high school biology teacher. In some ways our positions should have been reversed. Because for all my bookishness, I've always loved the outdoors. My husband on the other hand seemed to distance himself from nature by dissecting it and classifying the natural world. Now I think it was a way of coping with the largeness of the world. Looking at the small so that one isn't made dizzy looking at the large.

George and I were driving along the coast road one evening when suddenly he stopped the car. He just applied the brakes and without saying a word, walked across the opposing lane and went down the embankment. At first I was so confused that I thought I had fallen asleep and missed something, that we had hit a small animal or even a large animal . . . that some explanation was forthcoming. But then a car came and honked because we were blocking the lane so I pulled onto the shoulder and I began to be frightened. I got out and went down the embankment. And there in the sand at the high tide mark were his shoes. The light was fading but I could see him, swimming, far out. He wasn't much of a swimmer. I think I called his name a couple of times. Foolishly. And then he was gone. Just the waves dancing in the fading light. I stood there until it was completely dark and I couldn't see . . . then I took his shoes and climbed the bank and called the police. Well, the police were suspicious bordering on rude, but his body washed up the next day with no evidence of foul play and that was that.

My husband was a good man but there's a criticism of men implied in that remark. Was he "good" because he was better than I had come to expect from the general category? Or is "loving" something we do as an act of accepting the world into which we are thrown? That not loving someone or something would make life unbearable. And if we suddenly stopped loving, would that make someone take off their shoes and walk into the sea when they were not a strong swimmer?

From **The Man in the Hat** by Jeanne Beckwith

NAN: Old woman planning to move.

How many times do I have to tell you? I can't stay in this place anymore. It's haunted. When the ghosts move in, they never leave. I asked Father Dan to send them away, but he says they don't do exorcisms anymore. They get in trouble for doing exorcisms. God knows what else those priests get up to, but now they get in trouble for exorcisms, and the ghosts can just go on doing whatever the hell they want. I have talked to Miss Henry, and to Madeleine, and old Mrs. Flynn read my cards. They all say there's no hope for it. We have to move. If we don't move, then pretty soon, we'll be ghosts too. When the ghosts move in, they want company, and they don't take no for an answer.

When you were a little boy, you used to watch me sew for the neighbors. You used to stand there while I sewed and ask me how I did it. I told you the directions were on the package, but you didn't believe me. You just thought that somehow I knew. So, now let me tell you something I do know. I know that there are ghosts, and if I stay here, I'll be a ghost too. You want that? Do you want your Nan to be a ghost? Do you want me to sit here and become invisible? I used to drive a car down to the Stop and Shop. I used to buy cream buns after Mass, and we'd sit in the park and watch the people feeding pigeons. I can't do that anymore. I don't have a car. They took it away from me. I can't get out to Mass. The priest can't come and exorcise my ghosts. What kind of life is that? I'm afraid. I'm afraid this is all there is.

From **Integrity Problem** by Kevin Six

SUNEM WILLIAMS: A woman of indeterminate age and ethnicity, stands in a bathrobe and slippers with her hair in curlers. She smokes.

I tell you what. The police gots they selves a integrity problem. My man, Robert? He thought he'd make a good cop. Me too cuz he big, he don't take no shit off nobody, and I seen him shoot. He good. I told him, "I can just see you in that uniform shootin' people." That was before the integrity problem, when I thought cops cared about people.

So he go an take that cop test. Well, first thing, they don't give you a test. Oh no. First they make you fill out lots of paperwork and Robert? He just hate paperwork. Ain't no test neither, they just ax you a bunch of questions. But before they do that they make a big deal about Integrity.

"Baby," he say—He call me baby. "Baby," he say, "them police take the truth serious."

Good, I say. That fool need to tell the truth more. Like last week? Shit, never mind.

Just understan he never tell the truth, kay? But on this test, he tell the truth.

"Damn, Robert, I say. "You gonna be a cop in no time!" At that time I didn't know nothing bout that Integrity Problem the cops got.

Robert tell me about the Sergeant and how he told them for like a hour about how important it was to tell the truth and I'm like, "Damn!" And I wasn't even there. But then Robert tells me that after about a hour of this lecture then they get a, like, a hundred page form and they got to fill it out. So Robert fills it all out and tells the truth on every question, and he says there were some pretty easy questions to lie about, too.

"Like what?" I ask and he says, "Like 'did you ever commit a crime?'" And I'm like

"Shit," and he's all like, "Shit yes," and I'm like "and you told the truth?" And he said that it was pretty easy cuz there was just a box for Yes and a box for No—so it was pretty easy to tell the truth, he says.

So I'm thinkin' I gotta get me one a those boxes. I'm thinkin' our life's pretty good when That Asshole come and arrest Robert yesterday. I mean, shit! Turns out they didn't like Robert's answers to questions 172 and 175 and I'm like, "How many questions was there anyway?"

But this asshole's gonna ax the questions in person to be sure and Robert say, "I'm gonna tell the truth again." So that Asshole say: "Question 172: have you had sexual contact with a child?" And Robert say "yes but that OK, she legal now." Then the man say, "Question 175: Have you viewed or transacted child pornography?" And Robert say, "I ain't transacted anything but I seen it. You wanna see it?"

And I'm like, "Robert, don't go showing this Asshole any naked pictures of me!" But that Asshole just wanted to take my man to jail. And while they're takin' him away I'm just yelling, "But he told the truth! How you gonna' trust him he don't tell the truth?"

I tell you, the police gots a integrity problem.

Monologues for Men

From **Hey, Judae** by Ryan Buen

JOHN: 20 year-old male, simple and reserved.

Alright you really want me to say it, fine . . . you did this same exact shit with Tera and that's why you lost her. At some point you decided "Oh, I'm just not enough for her anymore, she's like this fucking Greek goddess that invented the olive salad" or whatever the fuck you thought made her so damn special. So you start making up all this bullshit, trying to be a guy that you were never gonna be. Do you remember when you bought that year's supply of pistachio nuts because she had a bag of them at her house one day? How about the time you started strictly drinking that shitty carbonated water because she casually mentioned once that maybe it tasted okay? How about that month where you listened to that shitty Evanescence cd every night because she liked one fucking song off of it. I swear, dude, if I heard the words "wake me up inside" one more time I was gonna puke. Do you think she didn't see right through that shit, man. Of course she stopped liking you, you weren't you. She started hanging out with you because she liked being around you, not some asshole that was gonna spend all of his time trying to impress instead of just being there with her. You fucked that up then, the same way you're fucking this up now. But you still have a chance here, bro, you can fix this. Talk to her, tell her what happened, give her the chance to forgive you, the real you. You owe her that . . . shit, you owe you that.

From **Boundary** by Tom Moran

TRAVIS: *Male, early 20s.*

You know, it took me a week to get into Canada. I was just going to go due north and cross up at International Falls. But I stopped on the south side of the bridge and just stared across it.

I watched the cars pass by and the river flowing and I couldn't do it. It was like a magnet was pulling me in the other direction. So I started driving west instead. I made it most of the way across Montana before I finally crossed.

And I just drove. Through Alberta and British Columbia. I kept pulling off the highway and driving through all of the little towns. I cruised through the neighborhoods and I tried to imagine myself living there, finding a job, starting a new life—maybe until the war was over, maybe forever.

But I couldn't see it. Something wouldn't click in my head. I kept pulling right back onto the highway, gassing up again, and before I knew it, there was another border. And for the first time since I left home, things felt right. So I crossed it, and I kept going until I ran out of road.

And then I got in a canoe. And I hid it in the woods and scammed my way into this place.

So was it worth it? Look around. Isn't this just like we always talked about? No draft boards or teachers or drill sergeants. Nobody here to give us orders. I'm living the dream. Right?

From **Revenge Fantasy** by Dawson Moore

GRIFFIN: Male, late 20s, bitter, trying to get his ex-girlfriend to leave his apartment.

So two years ago, I put this bumper sticker on the back of my car. It's the only one I've ever put on my car . . . I wasn't put on earth to advertise radio stations. This girl at the supermarket gave it to me. It said "Fall in Love," and I thought "What the fuck, why not?"

I didn't think about it again until you and I were six months in. When I realized what had happened, I was so proud: I had asked the universe for your love, and here you were. I had made all that new age horse shit work for me.

I just couldn't hear the universe laughing in the background. LOOK WHAT I'M GOING TO DO TO THIS STUPID FUCKER, it said to itself. I hadn't asked for a love that would last, or that would be honestly returned . . . I'd just asked to fall. And like I'd asked some lying-ass genie, the universe answered the letter of my wish, but not the intent. And this is where we find ourselves. You accusing me of a felony.

I am sorry that we didn't work out. And I'm sorry that my addiction to you has taken so long to pass. I know that's not convenient for you. Like it wasn't convenient for me that you moved on in a month, and didn't tell me. You let me find out through rumors and pictures you posted on the internet. "I love you, I want to grow old with you, I want to have your babies. . . ." Just nonsense. You imagine you're a fairy queen, but really, you're just a charming person with no interest in being anything more. I liked having sex with you. Now get the fuck away from me.

From **An Inexcusably Fantastic Theatrical Work Featuring Everything There Is To Know About Love And Absolutely Nothing Less Than The Finest Use Of The English Language To Describe Events Most Romantical by Ethan Cross, title edited to Everything And Nothing by Constance Wright** by David Clark

ETHAN: 20s. Male. Somewhat overdramatic storyteller. Recounting moments when he fell in love with a girl.

How do you just get comfortable and just sleep with her?
In a bed that small?
Really comfortable?
I don't know if you can.
Actually, you know, I'm not sure how it works exactly,
I think it's almost a mythic position to be honest,
but you're on your back, and she's lying on top of you,
her face resting on your chest, just at the neck.
If you lift your head up just a bit, you can feel her hair just slightly brush against your chin.
One arm is gently folded across her, and she grips you slightly with hers—the other arm can either hold her or just lie at your side.
She kind of overlaps you a bit on the side.
If it's done just right, you can feel her on you, but it's like she's there without being there.
You breathe just fine and it's fairly cool. It's kind of like a sleep nirvana or something.
I mean, I don't think I ever reached it.
Came close . . .
But only close enough to know if it just changed the smallest amount, we would be there.
But you can't change it.
If you try, you ruin what little you had of it to begin with.
(Moment)
Maybe. Or maybe the something I needed to change was the person I was sleeping with.
Perhaps the perfect woman is the one that you can simply sleep best with.

From **The Halfway House** by Cody Goulder

BENNET MILLER: Male, 20s, in love and hopeless

You know how in every movie made about romance, two people meet, lock eyes, and you know from that moment they're meant to be together? Well, we both know life doesn't work that way. If it did, no one would ever need blind dating services or those personal ads in the times. But, there is one case where the reality meshed with fantasy. I know it seems strange and awkward and uncomfortable for me, of all people to say this, but you mean the world to me, Jocelyn. When I look at you, I don't see a person, I see a marvel. And, I guess that's where the problem starts. Because of your beauty and your poise, I knew I'd never be able to stand up to you how I feel for fear of being shattered. I mean, how does someone go up to a muse and say you're their inspiration? Then, I heard you were leaving and it hit me. What would hurt more? Me never talking to you or me never telling you? You know, other guys I'm sure have ten times more courage than me, but they don't have my heart and I'm not telling you this so I can win your heart and you'll stay; that wouldn't be fair. I guess I'm tired of hiding behind a mask. Of holding back. But, most of all, I'm tired of always wanting you and never having the stones to do it. Now, if this were the fantasy, I'd tell you I love you and we'd embrace in a warm, passionate kiss. But, seeing as we're not and what comes of this, really, I don't care. All I will say is this. In whatever time you have, would you grant me the honor and cost me the small fee of a cup of coffee?

Teddy Berg's Story by Nicholas Walker Herbert

TEDDY BERG: 20s. A shy and nervous young man. Takes a bold step to tell Caroline how she's the girl of his dreams... on live television.

Hi. Uh. I've never done this kinda show before.
Uh. Yeah. Do I look over there... that camera?
Or over... yeah. Okay. Okay.

Uh. Hi. My name is Teddy Berg. I'm 29 years old, I like dogs, I work at a box company, and I like long walks on the beach. I mean, who doesn't like long walks on the beach? Maybe people in wheel chairs. Oh jeez, I'm sorry, I didn't mean to be offensive. I, uh, yeah. Sorry.

Um. Look. I don't really know if I can do this. I mean, not that I don't wanna be on a dating show, it's just... I don't wanna go on any dates. There's only one girl for me.
Caroline? If you're watching, I, uh. Okay... here we go...

This is what I would say to you Caroline, if I could have said it before your wedding.
I climbed the tree for you. I got stuck up there for you.
I waited by my locker every day for you to walk to math class.
I really liked you, Caroline... I... uh... I think I'm in love with you.
Is that a crime? If it is, I'm guilty. I'm more guilty than O.J. Can I say that on TV?

I mean, uh, I think I know what they mean when they say butterflies in the stomach?
They go nuts in there when I see you. When I talk to you.
And when I talk to you, I can see in your eyes, you're sad. And I don't mean like, um, I'm-gonna-slice-open-my-wrists-bleed-to-death sad, I mean like, you-got-mud-on-your-brand-new-dress, sad. I don't want you to be sad. If *you're* sad, then I know *I'll* be sad. You're sad being married to Joey. I know. He's my best friend. He's the biggest blowhard I know. Oops, can I say "blow" on TV? Oops! I said it again! Sorry! Sorry.

I hope you're listening Caroline. I hope. Cuz my 15 seconds of fame are up.

From **A Tribute to the Late, Great Bird** by Rand Higbee

MARK: A 25 year old baseball pitcher.

(He is standing on the mound looking in for the sign. He suddenly backs off and looks to the ball. He begins to talk to it.)

Come on, Ball. Big pitch. Need a strike here. Can't do this all myself. Going to throw you in the general direction, but you're the one that's got to get over that plate. Not too much of the plate! Just a piece of it. Just hit a corner.

A corner. The side of the plate. They call it the corner. Why? I don't know why. I guess because the ball only needs to go over a small piece of the plate to still be considered a strike. No, not going to get into a big discussion on Geometry. Just get over the plate. Hit a corner.

Oh, and one more thing. Very important. Cannot emphasize this enough. You must avoid the bat. If that big guy standing up there swings, you must avoid his bat. We clear on that one?

Why are you looking at me like that? It looks like you're smiling. Don't smile. This is very important. It's my career here. Take a look. Look at the stands.
 (MARK holds the ball so it can "see" the stands.)
Pathetic. No one. Three years ago I was filling up stadiums wherever I pitched. The Bird! The Bird was the word! I had it all! Now? Nothing. Nobody cares. He's just a loon. A crazy guy talking to a baseball. Haven't had a win in over a year. I really need this one. You've got to help me. Please? Please? You going to help me out here?
 (MARK gets back on the mound, gets his sign, then pitches the ball. He watches as it flies out of the park.)
Goodbye, ball.

From **Breathe In Breathe Out** by Gail High

DANIEL: About twenty five, committed to a mental hospital because he believes he killed his step-sister. After two year his guilt continues to torment him.

I look at the ceiling and I see Jesus, then another Jesus, then Sponge what's his name and a dog bone. Feeling crazy doesn't make it true but what do I know? They tell me—breathe in breathe out. So I do. Gaze at a green ceiling and eventually you are looking at yourself. You see the grass that was always greener, the money that was wasted, or the green Chevy you wrapped around a tree. You think about green frogs, green dresses with cleavage, green goats on Saint Paddy's day, painted on a dare. I'm haunted because I've never told the truth, the real story to anyone. But what do I know. My mind isn't like the movies where the past—days, months—are pulled up, filled with details. My past is sketchy at best, a splintered shell of what could have been. It's glossed over, dotted and enhanced all at once as if Warhol, Monet and Rembrandt had done a painting by committee. When all I wanted was a Rockwell.

Crazy wouldn't be such a bad thing. I could lose myself there, give up my guilt, just give up. But then I breathe in and breathe out. I can't hide from the true fact that I am not crazy. Breathe in, breathe out. Because if I were crazy this air would kill me with its innocence. Truth is she wore a tight red top every time, always the open cleavage, taunting me until she said yes to my no. Truth is she ruined me for any innocent encounters I would have found in my own time. Ten when she started on me—step-sister Mary—fourteen and the best tits anyone could ever want. But I didn't want them, not then, not ready. But truth is I'm guilty because, later, I did want them. Breathe in, breathe out.

From **The Chasm** by Laura Neubauer

JAY SWIFTFOOT: Mid-20s, recovering alcoholic.

You wanna know what my real problem is? It's not the booze, it's not the fights—it's you! You are a fucking leech. You've locked your sticky little self right to my back and it has sucked me dry. I try to pry you off but you stay stuck. I try to beat you off but just when I think I've won, you weasel your way back on. You're at my house on the couch. You come to my work and fuck around. I can't even take a shit without you asking how it went. But it's over—I want you out. Out of my face and out of my life. You know that night I almost killed you? That night I knocked you out—it wasn't an accident, it wasn't a drunken stupor—it was a decision, it was deliberate. I Bashed Your Brains and It Was Deliberate! Don't make me do it again.

From **Someone to Watch Over Me** by Jonathan Minton

LOUIS: Late 20s-early 30s.

(Louis and Laura have been seeing each other in what's become the ideal relationship for both of them. But Louis gets a job offer in D.C., and Laura doesn't plan on going with him. After a life-changing moment in a bookstore, Louis goes to Laura's apartment to see her.)

Something happened to me earlier today. You know how I'm not someone who just jumps into things, right? I'm usually a rational, logical person, I think things through, almost to a fault. Well I was in the bookstore looking at music, 'cause as if I would ever actually look at *books* in a bookstore. And that Ella Fitzgerald song came on, "Come Rain or Come Shine." Y'know the one, "I'm gonna love you like nobody's loved you, come rain or come shine." Do you know when the last time was I heard that song? Six months ago, here in this room at that party you and Jill were throwing. When I met you. I specifically remember it came on and I just happened to look up and catch your eye. You had two drinks in your hands, and you were wearing this red and black polka dot dress. That idiot Robbie was talking your ear off about aerodynamics or something ridiculous like that. And I caught your eye from across the room, for just a second, and you gave me this smile, the one you give whenever you read a poem or a book that you love. That's when I fell in love with you, Laura. Not when we were at the Italian restaurant with that rude waiter or that night we stayed up till four in the morning talking about Billy Wilder. It was that moment. And when I was in that bookstore, I actually *listened* to the song and what it was saying, and all I could think about was you in the red and black polka dot dress, and that smile. I can't just walk away from that, not for a better job, not for anything. I love you, Laura. And I know we've both been through a lot, but if you let me I'm . . . well, I'm gonna love you like nobody's loved you. Come rain or come shine.

(Beat)

I called Geoff in D.C. I'm not taking the job. I'm staying here.

'Course I Know Marcie by Eoin Carney

LEE: Mid 30s.

(Lee stands with a drink in hand. He still wears the protest clothing of his youth.)

'Course I know Marcie—we went to college together. I know what you're thinking: what's this guy doing coming to a wedding dressed like that. He must be really anti-establishment. Well I am, but I'll dress up when the occasion calls for it. Truth is I only found out about it last night and you don't wear a tux on the Greyhound. There's the poor sucker who's taking Marcie on.

He seems like an okay guy. Not what I would have expected. Can you believe she's a lawyer now? Time was if you told Marcie she would end up a lawyer she would have laughed in your face, right after punching it . . . She dragged me to this rally on the Mall once, to protest Clinton's welfare reforms. After it was over we decided to stay there all night—to show how serious we were. But the cops, they wanted us to leave the area so they could get things ready for some parade or dignitary or some shit like that. We told them NO. We were staying right there. We told them they could beat us, they could use tear gas, they could bring out the horses, but We Weren't Moving. But they went away, so it didn't come to that. Now we weren't alone together before you go getting the wrong idea. There were many of us—maybe six in total. We were like a family that night, all sharing the same dreams, the same resolve. I will never forget that night as long as I live.

(LEE exits quickly.)

From **Spring Tides** by Melissa Gawlowski

DREW: 30s, public school teacher.

(Drew's wife has just informed him that she has accepted a job offer across the country—against his wishes.)

You've gotta be kidding me. I've already moved with you once—I've built something here, Jane. Something I can be proud of. And just when I've finally got something here to feel good about, you want me to just abandon it? How many times are you going to ask me to start over?—Why am I a teacher, Jane? Why did I drop everything and start teaching—Have you forgotten I was something before that?—So we could stay together. You think it was easy, giving it up? You think I don't know what Meghan says about me, what they all said after I left the department? Do you think I like my old friends looking at me like I'm some dickless, balls-in-her-purse, pussy-whipped asshole? If anyone's the Tammy Wynette here, it's been me. I swallowed my pride, I gave up dreams, just to keep us together. And I found new things to dream about, to be proud of, I built it all myself. I can't keep throwing that away. I can't imagine you'd really ask that of me.
(Beat.)
Look. What matters is that I love you, and you love me, and that's bigger than anything. This Meghan-job's not everything. Once we get through the next year, things'll calm down, and you'll see, it'll all fall into place. We'll work out whatever—we'll get through it. Okay? I love you.
(Beat.)
I love you.
(Beat.)
See, that's your cue where you say—
(Beat. He waits for a response. It doesn't come.)
"I love you, Drew."

From **The Last Train to Hicksville** by Elena Hartwell

HYDE: The Husband, 30s. Suffers from PTSD from experiences in Somalia, Afghanistan, and Iraq. Grew up in Hicksville on Long Island—now living in Brooklyn.

What, Carle? How can you what? Keep coming over here all the time? It makes you so uncomfortable then don't. I never asked you to—I don't need you looking after me. I never asked for anything. You think I don't know you've been slipping cash to Angie along with the Saturday morning bagels? I never asked for that. I didn't ask you to come here. What do you want from me Carle? Don't get angry at me because I'm not reacting the way you want me to. I don't need your concern or your pity or your sweet rolls. Why don't you just head back to Manhattan. I'm sure you've got lots to do there. Why don't you worry about yourself for a change? I don't see you with a wife and kids living the American dream. You can criticize me but I can't talk about you? You don't think Angie and I talk about you? How none of your girlfriends stick? How you keep coming out here every weekend like a lost puppy looking for a little attention? You disgust me Carle. You're weak. You always have been. Crying like a girl. You may be the older brother but I had to take care of you when we were kids. You would have gotten beat up every day if it weren't for me. Four-eyed little geek that you were—still are for that matter. Maybe that's the problem with all your girlfriends- they should be boys—I'm sick of looking out for you—get out of here Carl "e."

From **The Virus** by Carolyn Kras

MAN: 30s.

Let me reassure you, I've had a funeral for my anger. I read *Transcending Hurt* cover to cover, and it's opened a lot of doors for me. I've forgiven how you sold my computer on eBay to pay your credit card. You needed a little extra cash. And totaling the Beamer. The car is replaceable, you aren't. The night I came home and saw you with the grocery bagger: Zap! erased from my memory. All of that's gone. And now I'm ready for you to move back in. Please, come home, I will lay out the welcome mat. Everything will be fine. More than fine: Fantastic. Because we've healed. And I . . . I really . . . Fuck this. No. Rachel, you were a virus. You somehow broke down my firewall, infiltrated my system, and all hell broke loose. Except I didn't know it until I was already half destroyed. Like those nasty Trojan Horse numbers. And it's taken me a long, long time to figure out how to quarantine your shit. I have re-booted my system. And now, you are permanently deleted. Find somebody else to infect.

From **Fire Dance** by Michael Parsons

SEAN MCMANUS: 30s, fireman.

(Sean is in confession, recounting a recurring dream to the priest.)

It's daytime. Sunlight is everywhere, I mean hurt-your-eyes brilliant. But I'm *freezing*. And the sun doesn't make me warm. So I build a fire. I rub two sticks together, and *whoosh*—I make a fire. Right downtown Chicago, Millennium Park.
> *(beat)*

I'm warming my hands over this little fire, and it feels good. Next thing I know, Nicky's there. He kicks sand on my fire. And he tells me, "no fires in the Park." And I was warm, and now I'm cold again, so I say, Fuck you—I'm sorry, Father—F-you, Nicky, I'm freezing. And he—he looks at me and says, "You've got it in you." And he takes a step back from me.
> *(beat)*

I look at my hand—smoke wisps start rolling out from under my fingernails. I take his arm—oh, God—and his suit catches fire when I touch him. It's fireproof, I know, but it catches fire. Nicky starts screaming and catching fire and it's on him now—his helmet's on fire, the picture he keeps of Dad inside the helmet's on fire, don't *ask* how I see it, but it is—and he's a sheet of flame. And as Nicky drops, Father, God help me, I feel the warmth, the heat of the flame coming off his smoking, ashen corpse—and I'm *warm again*.
> *(beat)*

And I like it.
> *(beat)*

And I do it again.
> *(beat)*

Everything I touch ignites. And I love it. Jesus Christ.
> *(Sean slaps his own face)*

Blasphemy.
> *(long beat)*

That's pretty messed up, huh?

From **Treefall** by Henry Murray

BUZZ: 30s-40s, a sober lumberjack afraid of heights.

(Buzz is the brother-in-law of the manager of a Logging Company. He has no affinity for either nature or logging and is afraid of heights. He has climbed the tree to deliver a contract to the tree-sitter protecting a Redwood. He talks rapidly to stave off the fear.)

I met my girlfriend in the program. We made eye contact for a year but she wouldn't have nothing to do with me 'til I got my cake. Smart lady. My first wife was a stupid-ass bitch. I went out over her. I'd been sober nine months, I was working and had us a nice apartment and something told me to go home for lunch and there was all this banging and she and her drug dealer, she was a crack head, were going at it in my bed. Well, I picked him up and threw him out the window and I wouldn't have gone to jail neither if she hadn't a said I hit her. I didn't, I just sort of shoved her off me. But that's not how I lost my teeth. The people in the downstairs apartment called the cops cause there was this naked man on the lawn cut up from the glass and his arm bone sticking up through his shoulder. The cops thought it was funny. I was only in jail about four hours. I went straight out and bought me a pint of vodka. I never drank vodka before in my life. Twenty minutes later it was gone and I bought another. Then I called my sister and told her what had happened and she went Buzz, if you can drive, get your hairy ass over her right now, so I said, I'm on my way. A year and a half later I showed up on her doorstep weighing ninety pounds soaking wet. Wet being my own urine. I was shaking so bad I couldn't even hold a cup of coffee. My sister fed me coffee from a spoon.

I went to see my first wife to make amends and you wouldn't believe how she looked. You think I look bad? When I married her she had this knock-out figure, pretty face, blond hair. It cost me a pretty penny each month to keep that hair blond. Now her face is sunk, her boobs are gone flat. She's still with that drug dealer. She looks like she could be your age. Uh, no offense. I mean, you been up here a long time and I want you to know I come to respect you a lot for a woman. I mean, you have really big balls and I believe they're brass.

From **Filmed in Bagdad** by Jeanne Beckwith

ABDUL SALAM: At least 35. A Middle Eastern man with his face half hidden by a scarf.

There are many like me, you know. We might remember bits and pieces from long ago, but not last week. How is this so? My friend, the man who found me, has a cousin who says I should tell the doctors the truth, but I am afraid they will lock me away. When you are locked away, you don't always come back. For now I will work in my new friend's bakery, and wait for my mind to clear. You say the movie you are making is a lie, but movies are different from real life. Movies are the stories that should be, not the stories that are. I would be grateful if someone could give me a story. Any story would be fine. The people who found me asked me who I was, and the name that I thought of was Abdul Salam. It was the only name I could think of. You are an actor, and perhaps very good at it. I wonder what I am good at. If there is anything that I love to do? Does it sound insane to you that I do not know? Sometimes when I am in the streets, the soldiers stop me. They think because I hide my face that I am hiding my identity, that I am a bomber myself. If only I had an identity! But then when I show them, when they see the scars, they pity me. I think they feel guilt. They give me chocolate as if I were a child, and sometimes at those moments, I do want to kill them, but those moments pass. I take the chocolates home and give them to my friend's children. They are happy to have sweets, and I am happy to be where no one can see me. At night, perhaps, I dream of who I was, but I do not remember. I do not think that I have dreams at all. That is hardest perhaps. Human beings live on dreams. We need new ones when the old ones fail us.

From **The Dollartorium** by Ron Pullins

MONEY MASTER: At least 35. Male. Quick to translate the world into the terms of business, power, and money. Donald Trump type.

(The MONEY MASTER has come to teach RALPH, owner of a modest corn dog business, what he has to do to make money in America today.)

You corn dog business needs a plan. A plan I can sell. Corn fields. Pig farms. Smiling pigs. Nice logo. As "organic" as a pig. Sunshine, corn, and pig meat. That's our corn dog.

Then smash the competition. First that frigging corn dog stand on the other side of town. Then corn dog stands in all the towns around—Leominster, Agawam, Pittsfield—until we have a chain of Corny Doo Doggeries. We buy out, shut up, run over, burn down any bastard in our way until we have Massachusetts. . . .
(Slaps desk)
Then raise our prices. And . . . I love this part . . . television. People love television. We hire publicity . . .
(Beat)
But what's the concept?
(Beat)
I got it. "Fun." Corny Doo Dogs are "fun." No. Not sexy enough. "If you want a big dick, buy a corn dog." Yes. But that lets women out. But, women want men with big dicks, so . . . we sell "Fun for men with big dicks and the women who love them." Perfect.
(Beat)
And. . . . it's American. Yes. Everything American. Red, white and blue, get out the flags, and fun, and big dicks. Then, ads at the super bowl and the Sweet Sixteen. Fun and flags, and girls where you almost see their tits, right? and you're there watching your TV and you think, oh, man, if she bends forward, you'll see her tits, and you watch, and you laugh, and that's fun, and flags, and red, white and blue. And this is fun for guys with big dicks.
(Beat)
Then onto Des Moines, and Kansas City. We get the product in stores, by the register, with flags, and, boy, is it fun, and the girl on television has her

picture by the register and you almost see her tits, right there in the grocery store, and men with big dicks think buy two, and flags, and fun.
(Beat)
And then we take it to Spokane. New Jersey. Baton Rouge—God fearing, Bible-loving towns which, if we get them, you get America, and suddenly we're in business, buddy, and it's time for Broadway, for the musical, with dancing corn dogs, and music, and fun, and flags, and girls swaying and if they sway like this you might just see a little tit . . .
(Beat)
Sell Corny Doo Dogs? No. We'll name it something like Xerox, or Coke, or Kleenex. But with sex, like . . . "Schlong!" But more American. Like "Pud." Puds! Pud Dogs. Puds House of Dogs. Pud this. Pud that. Puds. In the language. In the universe. It's why we live. God loves a good Pud and it's good to be an American.
(pause)
That's a plan I can sell.

From **In the Night Everyone is Equal** by Erica Silberman

JIM: Late 30s, a very wealthy man, and his wife Ali are entertaining Nikki, an old high school friend of his whom he hasn't seen in years, and her husband Gabe. Jim suspects Nikki and Gabe are there to ask for money for their new non-profit. Nikki has just slammed Jim for his lack of social conscience.

Don't "Hey Jimbo" me. You know it's true. You know, the problem with you liberals is that you're just as caught . . . you don't see that the same structure is applicable to you. Instead of flaunting money, you flaunt a moral superiority, protest marches, or organic food. Those are the luxuries of the upper middle class – the youth of the upper middle class. The big lie of the artist's life is that you all secretly want to be rich, but on your own precious terms. At some point in your life you have to admit that, and you resent people who are enjoying their lives. You have this thing about finding happiness in your work and being able to say, "Look at me, I help the poor." You know how you can help everyone? By being the guy we don't have to take care of.

Ali, please.

Your perception of us is solely based on justifying your failed philosophies, these liberal motifs that are supposed to make you happy, but don't. I'm not capable of that kind of a lie. We have a tendency to like the things we're good at and dislike the things we're bad at. Language and words weren't interesting to me. Money and human behavior were. My money, as messy as it is, keeps your little dreams afloat. Look down on me, but I went to school and got fancy degrees, and I'm all about how the world works, not how it should be. It's good to have these convictions until they actually cost you something. There is no clean money, and your boss's manners don't matter. If a drug dealer was going to give you a million dollars, you'd take it. If you had the courage of your convictions, you wouldn't. I'm freer than you because I don't have a lie to protect. Being poor isn't noble. Being a woman, a lesbian, poor, black . . . doesn't make you a good person. We're not equals. You come here looking down on us. If you had a million dollars you wouldn't be here. And you wouldn't be doing the shit you're trying to do. You want to protest me and ask me for money to do it. Doesn't that seem a little odd? If you're going to lie, do it with conviction. You're leaky, Nikki. You leak your contempt.

From **The Ugly Children of Eve** by Arlitia Jones

BILLY RAMSUER: Late 30s. A grieving father.

You'll forgive me, Father, if I doubt. That trusting servant of the Lord who used to open this door to you, he's gone. He's long gone. He's been lied on, tortured, deceived until his eyes ran tears and his heart swoled up with sorrow so big he couldn't carry it no more, had to lay it down, bury it in the ground along with everything precious he lost, everything the Lord saw fit to take away. That man used to love God and all creation, his heart is lying up on that hill with those four little griefs. At night I lean against this doorframe, watch the sun sink down the valley in a blaze of God's own glory, watch them four skinny crosses throw down their shadows in the grass. Think on that man. Faith ruined him. Man standing here now is all there is and I know one thing sure, any seed I beget on my wife is bound to come into this world early-marked for a grave. Knew that day you married us, to have and to hold from that day forward, I betrothed myself to suffering. Betrothed myself to her. My bride. My wife. My beautiful wife. When . . .

(Beat)

I kissed her. I knew it when I kissed her. She'd sucked a mint leaf before the altar. I could taste it behind the mask. Can't hide decay when it comes from inside you. She had a tooth going bad. In the back. Gave her much pain. Made her jaw tight. Rot, once it's in you, never goes away. Ma made apple sausage cake special for us. Lots of sage and cinnamon, the way I like it. My bride had no appetite, but I convinced her to try some. We ate with our hands, fed each other the way you're supposed to, shoved it in our mouths, smeared it on our faces till we were covered in cake. Drunk on spice. So I couldn't taste that rot. So I took her to bed. God forgive me. Found crumbs in her hair the next morning. I was careful, but I woke her trying to get them out. She went cross, said I was pulling her hair. I said "I would never do that. Never do anything to hurt you. Forgive me." Father, I love my wife. But I don't see it's my duty to beget a child on her again. I don't believe the Lord ever means to allow me to raise my own child in this world. Forgive me. I do not invite you in.

From **FleshEatingTiger** by Amy Tofte

THE MAN: Late 30s to 40s. Decent but looking scruffy around the edges.

(The Man sits center and smokes.)
There's this girl. Shit, I mean, woman . . . I've been seeing off and on for quite a while. Okay, maybe a week or so. I've seen her twice, alright? Fooled around in my car. Shit, like high-schoolers. Nothing serious. She's gorgeous. Perfect skin, great tits. Perfect. And she knows it. Wears little skirts that come down and show every move as she walks. These big full lips that beg to give head. I can't believe she's with me. I see the guys in the restaurant turning to check out her ass, her soft tan legs. She's a goddess. An absolute goddess.
(Beat)
Dumb as a fucking rock. I'm sitting across from her and can barely keep from leaping over the table and strangling her. The stupid, idiotic, shallow, boring CRAP that comes out of her mouth. WHO CARES?? And she doesn't fuckin' eat! She sits there picking at her side salad I paid eighteen bucks for and guzzles her Napa Valley chardonnay *right in front of me* like a fuckin' sieve. And all I'm thinking is . . . please be more interesting when you're drunk. Please develop a PERSONALITY. I'd really like to get laid, so please, be someone I can laugh with so I don't feel like a complete loser getting you drunk, fucking your brains out and never calling you again.
(Beat)
(Deep breath.)
(Beat)
But I can't shake this feeling. This tin can rattling in my head. I've dated a guy before. And I fooled around with a few guys. But only when I was drunk. I did everything drunk.
(Beat)
And when I feel it . . . It will be like walking together in the rain and not feeling the drops. Not like this. I won't feel like this anymore. I won't feel like drinking anymore.
(Beat)
I miss my wife, man. I really miss my wife.

From **Film Chinois**[2] by Damon Chua

EUROPEAN AMBASSADOR: Male, 30-50

When I first came to Peking, there was hope. It was before the war. I was young. I fell in love. Then the war came. I went back to Europe. I wanted to take her. But it wasn't possible. When the war ended, I came back, looking for her. I thought, now things will begin again. Lives will begin again. Time, which has stopped, will start again. The skies, which have been dark, will become light again. And I, who was incomplete, will become complete. But she was gone. I looked everywhere. I followed all the leads. Every one of them. Eventually I found out. She was dead. Killed by the communists. Killed by her own people, the same bastards who are now keeping me against my will. I promised her. I promised myself. I will never deal with the communists. Let them kill me. Let them.
(Long beat)
But I'm a coward. She's dead isn't she? What does anything matter anymore? We only have the living to consider. And that's the strategy isn't it: keep on living?
(Beat)
I gave her all of my heart. And now I have no more.

---

[2] By special arrangement with Samuel French, Inc. For performance rights please contact Samuel French Inc./Baker's Plays, www.samuelfrench.com.

From **Father Francis Gives His Farewell Sermon** by Joe Barnes

PRIEST: Middle-aged or older, at the pulpit, already a little drunk.

I cannot pinpoint the precise moment I lost my faith. There was no tormented dark night of the soul from which I emerged suddenly bereft of belief. There was just a day, nearly twenty years ago, when I realized I hadn't believed in God for ages. I felt no more sense of loss than I had, as a boy, when I discovered that it was my mother, not to the tooth fairy, who put that bright shiny new quarter under my pillow. I *did* wonder whether I should continue in the priesthood. But the truth of the matter was I really had no other marketable skills. There isn't exactly much demand out there for experts on the Albigensian heresy. Hypocrisy, it seemed to me, was preferable to hunger. So I decided to stick it out for retirement.

(Drinking)

Do not be angry at me for my false pretenses. And take comfort, if you will, in my fate. I will be spending my dwindling days in a home for aged priests. The furniture dates from the reign of Pius XII. There is the perpetual smell of antiseptic and urine in the air. The minds of most of my fellow clergy have long since drifted into the thin, drooling dreams of senility. I will be nursed by young men too stupid or effeminate to enter the priesthood. As you know, the church's standards in either category are not particularly high to begin with.

(Finishing his drink.)

And, dear brothers and sisters, *there will be no cable TV.*

(Looking at his watch.)

It is only twenty minutes to kickoff. And I appear to have come to end of the Johnny Walker. So it is time for farewell. I will not dawdle to shake hands at the end of the service. You've always hated it. And so have I. It is an unpleasant duty from which we are both henceforth released. I will leave you instead with a simple priest's simple blessing: May the Lord fuck you and fuck you and fuck you.

(Making the sign of the cross in the air.)

In the name of the Father, the Son, and the Holy Spirit.
Amen.

From **Ain't No Place Like Home** by Al Frank

PERMAFROST: 63 year old homeless man.

You think I was born under an overpass and been sleepin' in the weeds my whole life? You think I never had anything? I got out of the army and married my high school girl. I got college degrees. I taught writing at Montclair State College. I had a book of stories in the stores and a novel about to come out. We had a son, then a baby girl. She was pregnant a third time. We were paying off a house.

The life you know can vanish in a clock's tick. I went to meet with my publisher. She had a cab waiting to take me to the emergency room. The doctors kept telling me they were sorry. That's all I remember them saying and something about a car crash. I couldn't make sense of their words. Someone led me to the morgue. I stood before broken bodies that once held everything that meant anything to me. I couldn't breathe. The attendant said I should go home. I tried to get my mind around that. I left the hospital and walked all night. Over and again I repeated to myself, "I should go home". Morning came. I walked into a bus station and paid for a ticket. I don't remember to where. At the end of the ride I bought another. I drank whiskey till my money was gone. I threw my wallet in the trash. I couldn't recall my name. If someone asked, I gave the first one that occurred to me. That was the beginning of thirty-four years of using the ground for a bed and my sleeve for a pillow. I've never been back. I don't know if they were buried or turned to ash. Usually I don't answer questions about my life. But because I misspoke myself a few minutes ago I'm answering yours. No, I don't have a wife and children.

From **Engines of Time** by Jerry D. McDonnell

RICHARD: Late 80s to 90 years old. Retired railroad worker.

The depot's smaller than I remember. That's what age does. You get older, things get smaller. Used to be full of passengers and noisy than a fox rushing a hen house. Now it's quiet as death. Train tracks outside deserted. I've never lived anywhere else, past 80? 90 years?

I've had a good ride though. Two good wives and the stepdaughter's boy I raised after she left. The insurance gave up on all the medical bills on both wives and then me. Then they took my money. Put me in a room in a place that used to be a motel. Just a bed and a side table. A chair that no one ever sits in. The boy called the other day. It took a while to get me down to a phone. I could hardly talk. He said he'd come for me. The nurse said something about it being too risky. I figure I'll just take the train. Save him a trip.

(stands, points to the tracks in front of the stage)

But boy oh boy . . . in the day. Trains coming in and out. Those engines steaming in, wheels grinding and squealing, smoke stack screaming. I rode her all the way to San Francisco once. I remember going through the Rocky Mountains. Had never seen a mountain before. And then the tunnels.

Standing on that outside platform going through the tunnels it was like the train just dove into the earth and then popped back up. It was like life and death, heaven and hell, just took turns playing with you.

I painted the trains in the roundhouse. Paint lingers in my lungs like the devil laughing. Didn't know about masks in those days. You can't see on the inside what's on the outside.

(sits back down)

Those tunnels . . . got my ticket. Maybe get me a Pullman sleeper car. I earned it.

How'd I get here? Nobody else here. Just me. The train should be here any day now.

Stalker by Jaron Carlson

STALKER: A man of any age.

Sometimes I get close. Sometimes I watch from afar. I don't just watch one person either . . . I just simply watch the interesting ones. I mean . . . I seriously don't think there is . . . anything wrong with it. We all do it. I just make a habit out of it . . . and, yes, it is a hobby of mine.
> *(Beat)*

I like watching little kids. Mostly, toddlers. I know it sounds sick and I know you think I'm a terrible human being. And, I'm really sorry for sounding so disturbing but . . . you have to admit . . . kids are fun to watch. You can't honestly tell me that you don't agree because . . . they are.
> *(Beat)*

The best part is that they don't know any better either. They just stare. It's like they are the only ones who know . . . who know who you are and what you're doing there.
> *(Beat)*

I stared at a little boy for a long time once. Right into his dark brown eyes. He was playing in the playground in the sand pit and I was sitting on the bench just watching. I had a newspaper in my hands . . . and he was so ADORABLE. He kept looking up at me and smiling. And, of course, I smiled back. It went on for an hour or two before his mother picked him up to take him home. And, then I followed them. Every now and again he knew I was there. You could tell . . . I mean, he knew I was watching.
> *(Beat)*

I was just trying to make a connection . . . and, the connection is everything. The best part about "studying" kids is the connection.
> *(Beat)*

You see, for the rest of their lives they will remember me. Their memory of me won't be constant, or traumatizing or even life-changing, but every now and again I will be in the back of their mind.
> *(Pause)*

Just a flash . . . that's all it takes. Just a flash.

For Either Men or Women

From **Colleagues** by Allan Lefcowitz

A WORN DOWN PROFESSOR: Male or Female, 40s or older; jaded.

"We are such stuff/As dreams are made on, and our little life/Is rounded with a sleep." Ms. Anderson! In the presence of our greatest playwright might you refrain from popping your bubble gum. Thank you.

For the few minutes we have remaining, class, consider why Shakespeare wrote these lines for Prospero? Anyone have a thought? Does anyone know we are discussing *The Tempest*? Mr. Temple? Miss O'Keefe? Anyone? Ladies and gentlemen, semester's end does not mean "stop thinking." "End of the semester" means you ought to have reached that stage upon which you can think more precisely about Shakespeare's plays than you did at the beginning of the semester. Perhaps even share the professor's passion for them.

Over your beer and pizza, have you wondered why professors do this? It can't be the money. Perhaps respect? You will notice that Mr. Sheimerbach is packing his books while the last period has five minutes to go. And Ms. Anderson is still gnawing on her bubble gum. Could we teach for the intellectual stimulation and passionate sharing that one receives from alert students who suckle one's hard-acquired knowledge like—will someone wake Mr. Phillips before he hits his head on the desk and sues the college? You were just resting your eyes. As you do every class period. Has anyone the slightest glimmering of what Shakespeare felt when he wrote Prospero's concluding speeches? His passion is reduced to an ember. Prospero retires. Shakespeare retires to Avon. What should your professor do at the end of this most stimulating semester in which he has presented his intellectual tits for you to suckle upon? Oh, give you all an "A"? Very funny, Mr. Sheimerbach. Still what's an "A" worth anyway? Everyone will get an "A". Then again I might be crazy enough to give everyone an "F". "A" or "F". Behind one door a beautiful "A" is waiting to embrace you. Behind the other an "F" eager to eat your average. Ah, which door to choose. I have your attention now, do I? That's called dramatic tension.

Yes, Ms. Anderson? For the exam I recommend you study the plays of Shakespeare. Term papers on my desk by noon. Grades by Wednesday. Ladies and Gentlemen, I cannot say this semester has been a pleasure but

I will not speak ill of you when you are gone, nor make false report to the Dean. Yes, Mr. Sheimerbach, you may leave my presence. "Our revels now are ended."

And "My ending is despair."

The Dreamer by Barry Levine

DREAMER: A mental patient, either male or female, and of any age, provided he/she is still physically fit.

(The Dreamer is having a session with an unseen Psychiatrist.)

You analysts are always so hung up on dreams. And for what? To tell me I have a foot fetish or something—ah, who gives toenail decorated cake?

As long as I can remember I've always had very vivid dreams. You want to hear one?

The earliest one I can remember . . .?

I'm just a little kid and I dream that I'm awake lying on my bed in my room. At least it looks like my room but as I turn over on the bed and look across it this thing starts coming down out of the ceiling. No, not at me, just down from the ceiling to the floor. First is a large hand, with the forefinger pointing down, and the rest of the fingers and thumb curled up in a fist. After that there's stuff attached to it. I don't remember what kind of stuff, just stuff. And it's all attached together; all coming down from the ceiling to the floor. When it reaches the floor, it goes through it and disappears. And more stuff just keeps coming down. Sometimes it feels like the bed is moving up, except that as far as I can see it's still firmly on the floor. All the time there's this weird sound, like someone's humming "doo, doo, doo, doo, doo."

What do you think of that?

No! It's not a giant penis! I was six years old when I had that dream, maybe five! What kind of kid knows about sex at that age? Maybe I should rip your arms out of their sockets, whack your head off with them! How phallic would that be?

From **Pac-Man** by Tom Moran

BLINKY: A former videogame villain.

You think it was fun? You think it was fun? Bouncing around that stupid little box most of the time, only set free to follow you around. And right when we've got you, you turn the tables on us. Always the same endless pursuit down the same dark, tired corridors. Death was no escape, because there I am good as new five seconds later. And it never ended, the level numbers just changed.

And who got all the glory? You. And the money. And the magazine covers. And the chicks – including all the ones we never told Mrs. Pac-Man about.

And she deserved better. At least she sent us Christmas cards. Still does. Do you remember those electronics shows they'd invite us to? There you'd be signing autographs on the main stage, 500 people screaming your name, and we'd be stuck in some conference room panel discussion with a couple of Space Invaders and the snake from Q*Bert. And you would never even so much as wander over and say hello.

And now look at you, you broken-down sack of pixels. Fact is, you're down to your last life and I bet you're fresh out of quarters.

So I'm back to finish the job. Look at this as an act of mercy.

October 18, 2009 by Joe Barnes

THE SPEAKER: 20s-40s, male or female.

(The speaker is addressing his/her "ex.")

I'm the forgiving kind. I really am. I can forgive you the months of deceit. The lies about the long business lunches that you claimed to hate so much. The lies about those regional conferences that spouses never seemed to be invited to. The lies about that mysterious cell-phone that slipped out of the glove compartment when I was searching for a map. I can forgive you your betrayal, too. Your hours spent with someone else, sharing your body, sharing your secrets, sharing the life that I thought belonged to the two of us. I can even forgive you the cliché of the suitcase standing portentously by the door. And the oh-so-apologetic revelation that "darling, I'm so sorry but, well, there's someone else and I'm leaving and don't forget to pay the cable bill." But I will never forgive you for October 18, 2009.

(Beat)

You don't remember it? Of course you don't. It was just another drowsy Sunday morning in another wet October. I awoke before you did. I could feel and smell you even before I opened my eyes. Your back was against my chest, moist with a light sweat and heaving slightly. You skin carried the scent of soap and sex and sleeping animal. We were curled together so seamlessly that nothing—nothing—could ever separate us. And I was happy.

(Beat)

You know, I never expected happiness out of life. It was just something other people had, like twenty-twenty vision or perfect pitch. And I could have lived without it. Keep busy enough and you don't have time to notice that you're unhappy. But that morning, I was happy. You made me happy. Maybe for just a moment. But it was long enough. On October 18, 2009, you gave me hope. And now you've taken it away.

(Beat)

For that, love, I pray you rot in hell.

Contact Information

To inquire about rights to the monologues in this volume, or to request further information or scripts for the entire plays, please contact the playwrights directly at the addresses below, current as of the time of this printing:

Linda Ayres-Frederick, *Years Later: I Smell the Rain*:
   lbaf23@aol.com

Joe Barnes, *Father Francis Gives His Farewell Sermon; October 18, 2009*:
   jjbarnes@rice.edu

Jeanne Beckwith, *The Man in the Hat; Filmed in Bagdad*:
   rialto@tds.net

Paul Brynner, *Pivot Point*:
   slothrop@gci.net

Ryan Buen, *Now Boarding; Hey, Judae*:
   ryanbuen1@hotmail.com

E.J.C. Calvert, *The Bear (A Tragedy)*:
   http://ejccalvert.com/

Jaron Carlson, *Stalker*:
   j18carlson@yahoo.com

Eoin Carney, *'Course I Know Marcie*:
   eoincarney@gmail.com

Damon Chua, *Film Chinois*:
   nomadz@rocketmail.com

David Clark, *An Inexcusably Fantastic Theatrical Work . . .*:
   dwclarkpw@yahoo.com

Daniel Damiano, *Maya*:
   www.danieldamiano.com

Lillian DeRitter, *Discourse*:
lillian.deritter@gmail.com; @lillianlemoning (Twitter)

Al Frank, *Ain't No Place Like Home*:
moseful@hotmail.com

Melissa Gawlowski, *Spring Tides*:
http://melissagawlowski.com/

Cody Goulder, *The Halfway House*:
gouldercody@gmail.com

David Guaspari, *New and Selected*:
http://dguaspari.wordpress.com/

Daniel Guyton, *Where's Julie?*:
www.danguyton.com

Elena Hartwell, *The Last Train to Hicksville*:
www.elenahartwell.com

Corey Ann Haydu, *Café Manhattan*:
www.coreyannhaydu.com

Nicholas Walker Herbert, *Coming Clean*; *Teddy Berg's Story*:
nwherbert@gmail.com

Rand Higbee, *The Interview*; *Edith (that person in front of you at the coffee shop)*; *A Tribute to the Late, Great Bird*:
http://randhigbee.com/; rand.higbee@yahoo.com

Gail High, *Breathe In Breathe Out*:
gailhigh@mac.com

Arlitia Jones, *The Ugly Children of Eve*:
arlitia@arlitia.com

Carolyn Kras, *The Virus*:
www.carolynkras.com; carolyn@carolynkras.com

Allan Lefcowitz, *Colleagues*:
alefty@verizon.net

Barry Levine, *The Dreamer*:
blevine@usc.edu

Jerry McDonnell, *Back Home*; *Engines of Time*:
mcyukonjer@gmail.com

Jonathan Minton, *Someone to Watch Over Me*; *the Monkey Virus of Mildred Valley*:
jon_minton2@hotmail.com

Dawson Moore, *Revenge Fantasy*:
www.dawsonmoore.com

Tom Moran, *Boundary*; *Pac-Man*:
thomasmmoran@gmail.com

Kate Mulley, *The Tutor*:
www.katemulley.com

Henry Murray, *Treefall*:
henry.murray@mac.com

Laura Neubauer, *The Chasm*:
www.newplaysbyneubauer.com; laurajneubauer@yahoo.com

Michael Parsons, *Fire Dance*:
michael.s.parsons@gmail.com

Ron Pullins, *The Boss is Dead*; *The Dollartorium*:
www.pullins.com; pullins@pullins.com

George Sapio, *Headstrong*:
www.gsapio.com

Schatzie Schaefers, *A Fabulous Coat*:
schatzieplays@yahoo.com; 907-243-4653

Dennis Schebetta, *Green Eyed Monster*:
denschebetta@gmail.com

Erica Silberman, *In the Night Everyone is Equal*:
silberica@yahoo.com

Judd Lear Silverman, *Faith*:
juddls@sprynet.com

Lois Simenson, *Glaciers and Demons*:
simenson@clearwater.net

Kevin Six, *Integrity Problem*:
www.kevinsix.com

Judah Skoff, *Circus*:
http://www.judahskoff.com/; info@judahskoff.com

Kenneth L. Stilson, *The Cow and the Milk*:
kstilson@semo.edu

Scott Tobin, *Struck*: stob99@yahoo.com

Amy Tofte, *FleshEatingTiger*; *Roadmap of the Jilted Lover*:
www.amytofte.wordpress.com

Kavelina Torres, *Something In The Living Room*:
ekavelina@gmail.com

Karyn Traut. *Caffeine?*:
ktraut@nc.rr.com; 919-933-8791

Jennifer Williams, *Sexual Fantasies*:
jenniferhelenwilliams@gmail.com

Antoinette Winstead, *Refugee*:
awnyu87@aol.com

Index by Playwright

Ayres-Frederick, Linda; 40

Barne, Joe; 76, 87
Beckwith, Jeanne; 47, 69
Brynner, Paul; 34
Buen, Ryan; 14, 53

Calvert, E.J.C.; 35
Carlson, Jaron; 79
Carney, Eoin; 63
Chua, Damon; 75
Clark, David; 16, 56

Damiano, Daniel; 23
DeRitter, Lillian; 17

Frank, Al; 77

Gawlowski, Melissa; 64
Goulder, Cody; 12, 57
Guaspari, David; 38
Guyton, Daniel; 7

Hartwell, Elena; 65
Haydu, Corey Ann; 20
Herbert, Nicholas Walker; 19, 58
Higbee, Rand; 21, 41, 59
High, Gail; 60

Jones, Arlitia; 73

Kras, Carolyn; 66

Lefcowitz, Allan; 83
Levine, Barry; 85

McDonnell, Jerry D.; 18, 78
Minton, Jonathan; 8, 62
Moore, Dawson; 55
Moran, Tom; 86, 54, 13
Mulley, Kate; 15
Murray, Henry; 45, 68

Neubauer, Laura; 61

Parsons, Michael; 67
Pullins, Ron; 32, 70

Sapio, George; 27
Schaefer, Schatzie; 28
Schebetta, Dennis; 22
Silberman, Erica; 72
Silverman, Judd Lear; 36
Simenson, Lois; 42
Six, Kevin; 48
Skoff, Judah; 11
Stilson, Kenneth L.; 31

Tobin, Scott; 29
Tofte, Amy; 9, 74
Torres, Kavelina; 30
Traut, Karyn; 43

Williams, Jennifer; 37
Winstead, Antoinette; 25